MW00356441

VEGAN
PALEO

# VEGAN PALEO

Protein-rich plant-based recipes for well-being and vitality

Jenna Zoe

Photography by Clare Winfield

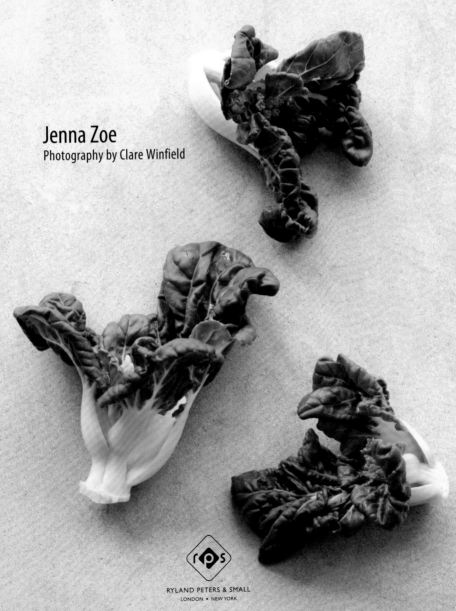

RYLAND PETERS & SMALL
LONDON • NEW YORK

**Senior Designer** Sonya Nathoo
**Commissioning Editor** Stephanie Milner
**Production Manager** Gordana Simakovic
**Art Director** Leslie Harrington
**Editorial Director** Julia Charles
**Publisher** Cindy Richards

**Prop Stylist** Jenny Iggledon
**Food Stylists** Jenna Zoe and Emily Kydd
**Nutritionist** Susan Church BSc (Hons), RNutr (Public Health)
**Indexer** Vanessa Bird

First published in 2015
This revised edition published in 2019
by Ryland Peters & Small
20–21 Jockey's Fields, London WC1R 4BW
and 341 E 116th St, New York, NY 10029
www.rylandpeters.com

Text © Jenna Zoe 2015, 2019
Design and photographs © Ryland Peters & Small 2015, 2019

ISBN: 978-1-78879-063-5

Printed and bound in China

10 9 8 7 6 5 4 3 2 1

A CIP record for this book is available from the British Library.
US Library of Congress Cataloging-in-Publication Data has been applied for.

## NOTES

• Both British (metric) and American (imperial plus US cups) measurements and ingredients are included in these recipes for your convenience, however it is important to work with one set of measurements and not alternate between the two within a recipe. Spellings are primarily British.

• Each recipe gives detailed nutritional information which is based on the largest serving size.

• When a recipe calls for grated citrus zest, buy unwaxed fruit and wash before using. If you can only find treated fruit, scrub well before using.

• There are many different brands of protein powders available and each have varying portion recommendations based on their specific blend of proteins. Standard scoop sizes vary (20–60 g/ $^{3}/_{4}$–3 oz.) but most brands provide a 1-portion scoop or list the portion size on the packaging. Refer to the packet instructions when following the recipes within this book.

• Ovens should be preheated to the specified temperatures. We recommend using an oven thermometer. If using a fan-assisted oven, adjust the temperatures according to the manufacturer's instructions.

• Sterilize preserving jars before use. Wash them in hot, soapy water and rinse in boiling water. Place in a large saucepan and then cover with hot water. With the lid on, bring the water to the boil and continue boiling for 15 minutes. Turn off the heat, then leave the jars in the hot water until just before they are to be filled. Invert the jars onto clean paper towels to dry. Sterilize the lids for 5 minutes, by boiling, or according to the manufacturer's instructions. Jars should be filled and sealed while still hot.

### Disclaimer

The views expressed in this book are those of the author but they are general views only and readers are urged to consult a relevant and qualified specialist or physician for individual advice before beginning any dietary regimen. Ryland Peters & Small hereby exclude all liability to the extent permitted by law for any errors or omissions in this book and for any loss, damage or expense (whether direct or indirect) suffered by a third party relying on any information contained in this book.

# CONTENTS

# INTRODUCTION

Here's what I know; thinking about food has us more confused than ever before. You would think that having a desire to live healthily would put you on the right track, but sometimes it can be quite the opposite. An interest in learning more about healthy eating can lead you further away from what you know works best for you. When new findings come at us from all directions, adjusting to the new, new can be a never-ending (and draining) endeavour.

My wish for you therefore, is that you take back the reins over your health and diet; don't hand them over to the experts, because only you will truly be able to discern what suits your body and lifestyle best. As a nutritionist, my job is to help people find their own way, not my way. Pay attention to what foods and which combinations make you feel good, great, and less-than-ideal. If you don't like the taste of avocados, you don't have to eat them. In fact, there is no one single food that's responsible for optimal health; it's about a variety of natural foods working in synergy to keep you functioning at your best.

It is important to remember that nutrition as an industry is still in its infancy; it's only about 60 years old. This means that every dietitian, health guru, and specialist is still learning, too. No one has all the answers and the goalposts keep moving.

The nutrition industry is often fragmented, and even within the plant-based realm, you have the 'no-sugar' camp ardently disagreeing with the fruitarians over which variety is best for most people, highlighting their differences rather than celebrating their similarities.

As a consumer of this information, it's important to remember that we are all on the same side. We all agree that whole, natural foods are the way to go.

No matter which foods you choose to include in your daily routine, you will feel your best if the bulk of your diet consists of fruits, vegetables, leafy greens and herbs, which is where the recipes in this book come in. There is so much more locked up in fresh produce than vitamins, minerals and antioxidants – compounds we don't yet know about because of the intricate relationship between the nutrients and how they work in tandem. Praising just one plant food for its nutritional benefits is reductionist and misses the point altogether. Feast on the things you love the taste of and cast the worry, the controlling and the calculating aside.

I also hope to instill the idea that eating well should not be dogmatic or a place to judge ourselves. Feeling vibrant and happy should be the only measuring stick. This book is intended to empower you to make healthy eating fun – but that doesn't mean you can't occasionally have your favourite food splurges and, in fact, you should. In the context of a healthy diet, there is room for any indulgence, whether that's a burger and fries or a slice of red velvet cake.

My hope is that the art of nourishing yourself becomes effortless and intuitive, so that your time and energy can be spent on more important things – living your life to the full!

With love,

Jenna Zoe

# WHAT IS VEGAN PALEO?

With so many diets out there, it's near impossible for any of us to decide how to eat. When you consider that proponents of every eating style claim their way is the best, the key to vitality and a lean physique, it's easy for us to try our hand at several of them, only to discover that they don't work for us. This often leaves us frustrated rather than empowered and confident in our own ability to make the best choices for ourselves.

I became vegan almost overnight on June 1st, 2009. Whilst I felt almost immediately better for it, it wasn't always upwards from there. There are infinite ways a vegan diet can look, and every time I read someone else's opinion on how to do it 'right', I tried it their way. I tried a macrobiotic diet and ate more grains and beans, I attempted a high-protein diet with the help of faux meats and soy cheeses, I believed the claims that you could eat whatever you wanted as long as it was vegan and still feel fantastic. None of these left me feeling my best.

At the same time, I was studying to become a nutritionist and reading a lot about the Paleo diet, which proposes eating only foods the cavemen ate for ultimate health. It recommends devising a dietary regime that includes whole, unprocessed foods, lean meats and low-carb foods that are high in fibre, potassium and healthy fats; and excludes grains, legumes, potatoes, dairy products, refined sugars and oils, and salt. Yet, it is still very possible on this plan to feast on bacon and dip your spoon into the almond butter jar with abandon, and wonder why your digestion isn't at its best, or that you aren't losing weight.

The healthy-eating world seems to split into those who promote a vegan diet and those who swear by Paleo. But what I've come to learn is that where these two diets overlap (with fresh fruits, vegetables, leafy greens, nuts and seeds) is where the real magic is. I truly feel that no matter what else you choose to eat, making these foods the basis of your diet is what leads to great health. They're fresh from the earth and bring with them the minerals they use to grow straight to our plates.

And this is where Vegan Paleo comes in, by combining the best of vegan and Paleo. I'm not here to sell you a new diet plan and this isn't a plan solely for weight-loss. Instead, this book is intended to provide you with fun ways to create meals that are largely composed of fresh produce, that will serve as easy blueprints you can play around with, whatever your dietary persuasion: if you want to add extra protein to one of these meals, or serve one with a side of brown rice, it's always ok to do that. The only thing I emphasize when it comes to eating well, is to get to know which 'extra' foods work for you. This is a no-judgment zone.

## Balance

You might wonder whether there is enough protein, or too much fat in this diet, or whether you can really get by without beans and grains if you're not eating meat. The answer is that only you can decide; the one-size-fits-all government recommendation doesn't take into account your specific needs. If you know, for example, that your body thrives on lots of fats in the morning, celebrate that fact and tweak your routine accordingly.

Alternatively, if you decide you want to fully embrace eating the Vegan Paleo way, that's great too. I have balanced every recipe in this book, making sure they are satisfying and filling, while still enabling you to feel light, energized and effortlessly maintain your weight. Throughout the book, I've made sure that the dishes are satiating enough to fuel an average adult and never too heavy or rich. This means that I've never gone overboard with the fats or sugars, just to make the recipe taste addictive. Instead, I look to fresh herbs, citrus and spices to add flavour.

My wish is that this book will help you get closer to your 'sweet spot'; the place where you intuitively eat health-giving foods most of the time, but also where you know how to make every bite taste delicious to you. I know that when I am excited about eating something that's good for me, I'm not left feeling deprived and wondering when it's ok to have a fall-off-the-wagon moment. Finding your sweet spot feels like being in cruise control compared to the stop-start routine of being really, really good and then, inevitably, really, really bad.

### Nutritional Information

For each recipe within this book I have provided nutritional information to enable you to make decisions on what to eat daily. It is provided as a guide and is an estimate only based upon the largest suggested serving. Nutrient values are derived from standard food composition sources, where available, but the actual nutrient content of the finished dish will be influenced by, for example, natural variation in foods, differences in processing and preparation methods, and the choice and weights of the ingredients used. The proportion of energy in a serving from fat, protein and total carbohydrate is also presented for each recipe. The percentage of energy from total carbohydrate includes the contribution from dietary fibre.

This information is intended to give an indication of the amounts of nutrients and energy provided by each recipe and needed for a healthy diet.

# Shopping for Vegan Paleo

To make a Vegan Paleo diet work for you, a healthy shopping basket is key; one that's made up of ingredients and not products. Eating was a straightforward practice of fuelling your body for our ancestors, and that's the way it should feel now – stress-free, fuss-free, and intuitive.

Start with fresh produce of all kinds; not only fruits, vegetables, and leafy greens, but herbs and seaweeds too. Think of your health as an asset and invest plenty of time in getting to know the plant foods that you love. I advise clients to come up with a list of their five favourite fruits and vegetables, then to make these mainstays on their shopping list so that it's always possible to assemble something to eat quickly that they'll enjoy. My favourites are bananas, kale, parsley, artichokes and red onion. Get to know which ingredients you don't like, too. Good health doesn't come from singular foods or nutrients, but from a variety of them working in synergy.

Avocados. These are technically a fruit but deserve identification on their own because when putting meals together, you should count these as a fat in the same way you would with nuts, seeds and oils. I regularly count on half an avocado to bulk up a salad and increase satiety. Regularly eating avocado also has huge beauty benefits and can be more powerful at keeping breakouts at bay than any pill or cream!

Nuts are vital in a Vegan Paleo diet. Try almonds, macadamia nuts, pine nuts, brazil nuts, pistachios, walnuts, the list goes on. The only nut to minimize is the cashew, which are comparatively inexpensive and blend easily, so raw and vegan recipes often over-rely on them for creaminess and texture, but I avoid them on the whole because they can encourage the formation of yeast in the body. If you have a tendency towards candida or a weak digestion, cashews are best left alone. Additionally, we have largely excluded peanuts in this book because they are technically a legume rather than a nut, which renders them not strictly Paleo. If you feel confident enough to play around with certain borderline ingredients and make a decision based on how eating them makes you feel, go right ahead.

One word about nut consumption: it's oh, so easy to overdo it, especially if you're munching on them mindlessly, so take care. The consensus is that one serving of nuts is about 30 g/1 oz., which translates as 22 almonds, 40 pistachios or 14 walnuts. I don't portion them out *per se*, but it can be a useful habit to practice until you can safely eyeball the right amount for you.

Consider seeds the way you would nuts and snack on a small handful from time to time. Adding a heaped tablespoonful to a main meal will help you effortlessly hit your recommended daily intake for fats. There are 'it' seeds like chia and hemp, but don't forget about the less glamorous ones. I love snacking on toasted pumpkin seeds for zinc, and tahini, made from sesame seeds, is a great way to get calcium without dairy.

Coconut products: desiccated/shredded, water, oil, the flesh, are all healthy and a deliciously easy way to add flavour!

Other healthy oils include olive, flax, sesame, pumpkinseed and avocado oil. Less healthy choices include canola, grapeseed, soybean, and corn oils, plus any oils that are labelled 'vegetable oil'. I recommend avoiding products that list hydrogenated or partially-hydrogenated oils as one of their components: these contain carcinogenic trans-fats that are harmful to our bodies because their chemical structure has been altered during a heating process. It's common knowledge that oils are calorie-dense (100–120 calories per tablespoon) and for that reason we're told to show restraint. Personally, I'm not scared of adding lashings of olive oil to dishes, but most of the time I keep in mind that oils are still processed in some way and so not as healthy as whole fats. What this means is that given the choice, I opt for avocado over avocado oil, olives over olive oil and ground flaxseeds instead of flax oil. Think of oils as condiments.

Pseudograins are a group of foods that resemble grains in the way humans consume them, but aren't actually grains. Namely, we're talking about amaranth, quinoa and buckwheat. Biologically, they aren't really grains at all (in the way that wheat, rye and barley are), but rather seeds of broadleaf plants. They are gluten-free, contain fewer carbohydrates than regular grains and are more nutrient-dense. People disagree over whether pseudograins merit inclusion in a Paleo diet, but I think they are right for some people and not others.

# Essential Ingredients

## Hemp Seeds

When people worry about getting enough protein on a vegan diet, I direct them straight to hemp seeds, a complete protein, containing all 8 essential amino acids. They blend well, without soaking or sprouting, and offer a nut-free way to make milks and creams.

## Chia Seeds

There is no one perfect food but these tiny Titans come pretty close: a complete protein, rich in omega-3 fats, a wide array of minerals and loads of fibre to boot. Aside from the fact that they are nutritional superstars, you can make 'chia eggs' by mixing them with a little water that legitimately replaces the real thing in baked goods and treats.

## Spirulina

Spirulina's chlorophyll content is way higher than regular greens, which makes it an excellent detoxifier and blood cleanser. Like chia and hemp seeds it is a complete protein, so sprinkling a teaspoon or two over salads is a handy way to up protein consumption.

## Coconut Oil

Coconuts are rich in medium-chain triglycerides, the healthy kind of fat that helps regulate the thyroid gland, which in turn regulates metabolism. It's an excellent choice for cooking with as it doesn't hydrogenate or turn into a trans-fat very easily.

## Nuts (but not peanuts)

Nuts are handy when you want to create creaminess in a dressing, or make non-dairy cheeses, dips, pâtés, or milks. I find that macadamia nuts, pine nuts and almonds are the most versatile but use any you like.

## Cacao Nibs and Raw Cacao Powder

This is your chocolate fix in its purest form, and it's oh, so healthy! Not only does cacao satisfy chocolate cravings, but it delivers a great boost of magnesium, calcium and iron, which makes it a highly alkalizing food, too.

## Nutritional Yeast

This ingredient will provide a cheese-like taste to your cooking without resorting to dairy. It also contains the complete spectrum of B vitamins, which our bodies burn through more quickly when we are stressed.

## Apple Cider Vinegar

This is the only vinegar that is technically alkaline, which has a soothing effect on digestion. Additionally, if you buy a brand that's raw or contains a starter culture it will have probiotic benefits.

## Grain-free Flours

If you like to make your own treats, get to know these flours, whether it be almond-, quinoa-, or buckwheat-based. They all behave slightly differently, but you can substitute them in all of your favourite bakes for gluten-free variations.

## Quinoa

You may decide that you want to exclude pseudograins from your diet entirely, but if you allow one exception, keep quinoa. It's 14% protein, super-versatile and very filling.

# Vegan Paleo Parameters

This book is not meant to offer a restrictive way of eating; I encourage you to figure out which foods suit you and adjust the guidelines accordingly. It's all about what works best for your body and your lifestyle. Like I said, this is a no-judgment zone.

## What to Avoid

### Salt

I'm not in the business of giving weight-loss advice, but I do believe that eating too much sodium contributes to water retention, especially for women. It's entirely possible to eat a healthy diet but overdo it on the salt and wonder what's causing that extra puff. Too much sodium wreaks havoc on the natural mineral balance in the body and it can be dehydrating. For this reason, I keep salt to a minimum, only adding in a little where I think the recipe really benefits from it, but you can always season with salt to taste.

### Free-from Foods

Fat-free muffins, gluten-free biscuits, free-from pastas, foods labelled 'free-from' are usually gimmicky and not very healthy. I say usually though because that's not always the case. As a rule of thumb, if they are made of mostly corn products, soy products and sugars, they aren't the guilt-free treats they promise to be.

### Refined Sugars, Flours and Grains

White sugar and plain/all-purpose and self-raising/rising flours mess about with our digestion because or bodies don't know what to do with them. Not only do they upset the balance of good bacteria in the gut, they are also anti-nutrients that strip the body of valuable minerals. Additionally, they are recognized by our bodies as a toxin and are therefore more likely to be sent straight to our fat cells for storage. If the product also contains gluten (meaning wheat, rye, spelt, most oats and barley or their flours), it will also have an inflammatory effect on the body and will exacerbate any existing chronic symptoms you may be experiencing.

### Dairy

I have completely omitted dairy from this book; not only is it excluded from both vegan and Paleo dietary guildelines, but, as I tell all my clients, it's intended for baby cows! Most of us are unable to digest dairy because it is not designed for human consumption.

## What to Consider

### Beans, Pulses and Legumes

These are not part of a Paleo eating plan for a number of reasons, so are excluded from the recipes in this book. Primarily, beans and pulses contain compounds called phytates, which prevent us from absorbing the minerals in foods. They also contain lectins which can cause inflammation in the stomach, leading to 'leaky gut syndrome'. A lot of people don't digest this group of foods well, and have to deal with bloating and discomfort when consuming them. Of course, if you'd like to supplement your eating plan with beans and pulses and find that they don't mess up your digestive system, include them, but if you are looking to be strictly Paleo, then avoid chickpeas, broad/fava beans, lentils, peanuts, etc. altogether.

## Whole Grains

Similarly, we have also excluded whole grains entirely as they aren't strictly Paleo, but if you find they really suit you, feel free to keep them in your diet.

## Simple Substitutions

There are a handful of ingredients that feature in the recipes in this book that may be hard to find, more expensive than others, or that you'd prefer not to use. Where this is the case I've offered alternative ingredients that work just as well in each recipe. For example, Bragg liquid aminos can be easily substituted with soy sauce, and honey can be substituted with agave or maple syrup.

## Treat Strategies

I encourage my clients not to associate their habits with morality – giving into a craving once in a while doesn't make you a bad person, nor weak-willed. If a healthy diet is about making good choices 80% of the time, there is space for a guilty pleasure, no matter what it is, in the other 20%. If having a deep-fried meal once a month keeps you on track the rest of the time, go for it.

Let's face it: we live in a fast-paced world and need to use some shortcuts to save on time. Things like non-dairy milks, nut butters, and dark/bittersweet chocolate are technically processed foods, because they have been altered from their original state, but minimally so, and it's unrealistic to expect that we won't rely on these kinds of staples from day to day. It's a question of to what degree.

And, while we're at it, alcohol is a processed food but it's an unavoidable part of life for many of us. Within this realm, there are bad, better and best choices you can make. If you're buying wine for example, it's becoming easier to seek out organic and sulfite-free brands. Like with any health change, it's about choosing better, most of the time. There is no need to go without anything all of the time in the quest to feel good.

Indulging in treats is a necessary part of life; after all, eating is not only needed to make your body happy but your soul happy too. To my mind, most of us fall into two distinct camps when it comes to indulging; the people who like to have a small treat each day and the people who prefer to stay focused on healthy eating most of the time, saving their wiggle room for a blow-out treat. Both of these are good strategies, so it's about deciding which one works for you. For example, I prefer a small treat each day, but that doesn't mean I'll turn down ice cream cookie sandwiches for a special occasion as well.

# SUNRISE START

To me, breakfasting like a king means making the first meal
the most nutritious it can be. It's the one that quite literally
teaches our hormones how to behave for the rest of the day,
affecting our energy levels, our metabolism and our mood.
Our ability to make conscious decisions is also at its strongest
in the morning, so when you start your day on the right foot,
staying in that healthy groove will feel like *way* less effort.

# Trio of tonics

## Turmeric tonic

1 teaspoon turmeric powder
2 teaspoons lemon juice
a 5-cm/2-inch piece of ginger,
    peeled
a pinch of salt
a pinch of ground black pepper
stevia, to taste
1 cup ice cubes

## Date-orade

375 ml/1½ cups coconut water,
    chilled
2 fresh dates, pitted
a few drops of pure vanilla
    extract
a pinch of pink Himalayan salt,
    to taste

## Carob latte

375 ml/1½ cups almond milk
1 tablespoon decaffeinated
    espresso powder (or Dandy
    Blend)
1½ teaspoons carob powder
a few drops of pure vanilla
    extract
a pinch of pink Himalayan salt
1 teaspoon clear honey, agave
    or maple syrup (optional)

*a juicer*

## Each Serves 1

Substitute your morning tonic, energy drink or coffee with one of these tasty treats to make your day a little bit healthier. Turmeric is a great anti-inflammatory, so, as well as adding it to soups, dressings and curries, I also love to drink it in tonic form. My Date-orade provides the perfect amount of 'pow' for an intense workout; the coconut water and salt balance out the lost liquids and sodium from a hard sweat. And whether you drink coffee or not, the ritual of taking a break is great for the soul. Go java-free with a Carob Latte!

## Turmeric tonic

Extract the juice of the ginger using a juicer (you need about 1 teaspoon). Transfer to a mixing jug or shaker with the remaining ingredients and 250 ml/1 cup of water. Stir well, pour into a glass and serve immediately.

## Date-orade

Put all of the ingredients in a blender and blend until smooth and frothy. Pour into a glass and serve immediately

## Carob latte

Gently heat the almond milk in a saucepan or pot set over a medium heat. Put the remaining ingredients in a mixing jug or shaker and stir or shake until well combined. Add the warm almond milk and stir or shake again. Serve immediately. You can also make an iced latte by mixing all the ingredients together in a mixing jug or shaker, without warming the almond milk, and adding ½ cup of ice cubes.

---

### NUTRITIONAL INFORMATION

**Per Turmeric Tonic:** 6 kcals/27 kJ, 0.3 g fat (0.1 g saturated), 0.4 g protein, 0.6 g carbs (0.3 g sugars), 0.5 g salt, trace fibre
**Per Date-orade:** 154 kcals/653 kJ, 1.2 g fat (0.8 g saturated), 2.2 g protein, 32.5 g carbs (32.5 g sugars), 1.6 g salt, 1.2 g fibre
**Per Carob Latte:** (if using honey) 141 kcals/592 kJ, 4.1 g fat (0.4 g saturated), 2.8 g protein, 19.6 g carbs (19.2 g sugars), 1 g salt, 6 g fibre

# Trio of Protein Shakes: Maca, Mocha, Matcha

You can get enough protein in a plant-based diet, but good-quality protein powders act as a nice cover, especially on days when you're too busy to think about it. These are my favourite weekday breakfast drinks because they taste like a treat, but I know I'm providing my body with what it needs.

## Maca

375 ml/1½ cups almond milk
1 scoop protein powder (see page 4 for information on serving sizes)
½–1 teaspoon maca powder
¾ cup ice cubes
¾ teaspoon xanthan gum

## Mocha

375 ml/1½ cups almond milk
1 scoop protein powder
1 tablespoon raw cacao powder
40–55 ml/1½–2 oz. espresso or 1 tablespoon espresso powder
1 frozen banana (see page 22)
½ cup ice cubes
¾ teaspoon xanthan gum

## Matcha

375 ml/1½ cups almond milk
1 scoop protein powder
½ teaspoon pure vanilla extract
1 teaspoon matcha powder
¾ cup ice cubes
¾ teaspoon xanthan gum

*a high-speed blender*

ALL SERVE 1

Each of these smoothies can be made in the same way. Start by putting the almond milk in a blender with all the ingredients except the ice and xanthan gum. Blend to combine, then add the ice and xanthan gum. Blend again and watch the texture transform while the liquid goes around.

You'll end up with a thick and delicious protein shake that can be served in a glass or poured into a flask to take with you on the move.

---

### NUTRITIONAL INFORMATION

**Per Maca Shake:** 201 kcals/842 kJ, 5.1 g fat (0.4 g saturated), 19.3 g protein, 14.3 g carbs (12.5 g sugars), 1.1 g salt, 10.1 g fibre
**Per Mocha Shake:** 366 kcals/1536 kJ, 9.3 g fat (2.8 g saturated), 24.7 g protein, 38.8 g carbs (31.3 g sugars), 1.5 g salt, 13.8 g fibre
**Per Matcha Shake:** 208 kcals/873 kJ, 5.4 g fat (0.4 g saturated), 20.1 g protein, 13.2 g carbs (11.7 g sugars), 1.1 g salt, 10.7 g fibre

# Green-a-Colada

Confession: I won't eat or drink something healthy if it doesn't taste delicious to me. I want every bite to delight my tastebuds because that's my number one tip for never feeling deprived. If you can identify with this, these are the kinds of green smoothies for you.

400 g/3 cups pineapple, cut into chunks
1 banana, peeled
500 ml/2 cups coconut water
150 g/3 cups spinach (frozen or fresh)
1 tablespoon coconut oil (optional)
sliced fresh pineapple, to serve

## To Serve (optional)

2 tablespoons hemp seeds
2 tablespoons desiccated/ shredded coconut

## Strawberry Shake

1 large chard leaf, de-stemmed
375 ml/1½ cups almond milk
1 frozen banana (see method)
6 strawberries, fresh or frozen
1 tablespoon almond butter
½ teaspoon pure vanilla extract
stevia, to taste
1 cup ice cubes
½ teaspoon xanthan gum (optional)

*a high-speed blender*

## Serves 2–4

Put the pineapple and banana in separate freezer bags and freeze for at least 8 hours, or overnight.

Put the coconut water in a blender with the frozen pineapple, frozen banana, spinach and coconut oil (if using). Blend until completely smooth.

Pour the smoothie into two tall glasses or four smaller glasses to serve. Top each with hemp seeds and desiccated/ shredded coconut if desired, or, for added extravagance, put a slice of fresh pineapple on the rim of each glass.

## Strawberry Shake

Green drinks needn't be green-coloured. Put the chard in a blender along with the rest of the ingredients and blend until smooth to make a healthy green drink disguised as a Strawberry Shake.

> **NUTRITIONAL INFORMATION**
> Per serving: 418 kcals/1752 kJ, 15.7 g fat (8.6 g saturated), 10.4 g protein, 53.9 g carbs (49.4 g sugars), 1.1 g salt, 9.9 g fibre
>
> *For Strawberry Shake, see page 141*

# Heart-opening Shake

I am a chocoholic – I love the stuff, and luckily there's no reason to give it up. It's high in magnesium and iron, and cocoa is a vasodilator, meaning it relaxes our blood vessels, causing them to expand. This is why chocolate is associated with romance and love so often – it literally opens up the heart and all that flows through it!

**375 ml/1½ cups hemp milk**
  **(see Tutorial below)**
**100 g/½ cup fresh figs**
**1 frozen banana (see page 22)**
**1 tablespoon almond butter**
**1 tablespoon raw cacao powder**

*a high-speed blender*

## Serves 1

## Hemp Milk
**60 g/½ cup shelled hemp seeds**

## Makes 500 ml/2 cups

First, prepare the hemp milk following the Tutorial below. There's no need to make this in advance for this recipe, but I find it's a good ingredient to have to hand and keeps in the fridge for up to 2 days once made.

Pour the hemp milk into a blender. Cut the figs into quarters using a sharp knife and add to the milk with the frozen banana, almond butter and cacao powder.

Blend all the ingredients together until completely smooth.

Pour into a glass and serve with a straw.

## Tutorial: How to Make Hemp Milk
Put the hemp seeds in a blender with 375 ml/1½ cups of water and blend on a high setting until completely smooth. The hemp seeds contain no enzyme inhibitors so they don't need to be soaked prior to blending, and they blend in so easily with the water that there is no need to strain the milk through a fine mesh sieve/strainer, like you usually have to with other nut and seed milks. The ratio here is key, so if you want to make more milk than this recipe yields simply ensure you combine 1 part hemp seeds with 3 parts water.

> **NUTRITIONAL INFORMATION**
> **Per serving:** 608 kcals/2535 kJ, 34.6 g fat (5.2 g saturated),
> 25.5 g protein, 42.3 g carbs (30.5 g sugars), 0.5 g salt, 12.8 g fibre

# Pear and Cranberry Muffins

1 tablespoon psyllium husk powder (or regular whole psyllium husks ground using a coffee grinder)

200 ml/³⁄₄ cup almond milk

30 g/¹⁄₄ cup hazelnuts

110 g/1 cup almond flour

20 g/¹⁄₄ cup desiccated/shredded coconut, plus extra for sprinkling on top

¹⁄₂ teaspoon pure vanilla extract

1¹⁄₂ tablespoons coconut oil

1 medium pear, peeled, cored and diced

4 tablespoons unsweetened dried cranberries

*a 6-hole muffin pan lined with squares of baking parchment*

Makes 6

The biggest factor in transitioning to a healthier diet successfully is doing so without feeling like it's too much of a move away from your current lifestyle. If you're a grab-a-muffin-and-run-out-the-door kinda person, that morning ritual doesn't need to be thrown out. Just upgrade the muffin in question, and continue to enjoy the extra lie-in time you so love.

Whisk the psyllium husk powder and almond milk together in a large mixing bowl and set aside, allowing the mixture to thicken.

Pulse the hazelnuts in a food processor until a fine powder has formed but some chunks still remain. Combine the ground hazelnuts with the almond flour and desiccated/shredded coconut in a separate large mixing bowl.

Pour in the almond milk mixture, the vanilla and the coconut oil, then stir. Cover and set aside for at least 1 hour to allow the batter to rest.

Preheat the oven to 180°C (350°F) Gas 4.

Fold the diced pear into the batter, along with the cranberries.

Pour the batter into the lined muffin pan, sprinkle with a little extra desiccated/shredded coconut and bake in the preheated oven for 1 hour, or until the muffins have firmed up.

Remove the pan from the oven and allow the muffins to cool slighty before serving.

### Top Tip

These muffins are perfect for slicing in half and spreading with applesauce or your favourite Sweet Spread (see page 33).

### NUTRITIONAL INFORMATION

**Per muffin:** 233 kcals/971 kJ, 10.8 g fat (4.7 g saturated), 8.7 g protein, 20.4 g carbs (17.5 g sugars), 0.1 g salt, 9.2 g fibre

# Acai Bowls Galore

Having an acai bowl literally feels like eating ice cream for breakfast, and there are loads of fun ways to make them. If you are making these bowls for children, set up a toppings station and let them pick their own; it's a great way to start getting them more connected with what's going into their bodies. Acai is one of the only fruits that contains Omega-3 fatty acids, it has double the antioxidants of blueberries and is fantastically energizing. All you have to do is blend the base until smooth, and then top with whatever you like. Look for puréed acai packs in the frozen section of your grocery store, or else you can also go for the powdered version.

**1 pack frozen acai purée**
   **(about 100 ml/$\frac{1}{3}$ cup)**
**1 frozen banana (see page 22)**
**200 ml/$\frac{3}{4}$ cup almond milk**

## To Serve

**20 g/$\frac{1}{4}$ cup desiccated/**
   **shredded coconut**
**goji berries**
**strawberries, sliced banana**
   **or kiwi (optional)**

## Serves 2

Put the acai purée, frozen banana and almond milk in a food processor and blend together until smooth.

Pour the mixture into bowls and sprinkle with desiccated/shredded coconut and goji berries. Serve with fruit – a variety will work well here; try strawberries, banana or kiwi slices.

## Variations

There are many ways to make this bowlful of goodness. Substitute the acai purée for 5 frozen strawberries and top with extra strawberries and cacao nibs, or use 30 g/$\frac{1}{4}$ cup frozen blueberries instead of the acai purée and top with sliced kiwi and coconut chips. For an extra thick fruit base, add an extra frozen banana, or try blending in 2 teaspoons of cacao powder, then top with almond butter and hemp seeds for a chocolate and nut variation.

Other fun toppings include a handful of grain-free granola, a dollop of yogurt (such as the Coconut Yogurt on page 34), crushed seeds and nuts, or any sliced fruit you desire.

> **NUTRITIONAL INFORMATION**
> **Per serving:** 221 kcals/922kJ, 10.7 g fat (6.3 g saturated),
> 3.9 g protein, 23.8 g carbs (21.7 g sugars), 0.2 g salt, 7.1 g fibre

# Paleo Pancakes with Date Caramel

80 g/scant ¾ cup almond flour

40 g/¼ cup arrowroot starch

1 teaspoon baking powder

½ teaspoon ground cinnamon

a pinch of salt

1 tablespoon xylitol or
    granulated stevia

4 tablespoons apple purée/
    applesauce

½ teaspoon pure vanilla extract

1 tablespoon coconut oil, plus
    extra for greasing the pan

60 ml/¼ cup almond milk

100 g/1 cup mixed fresh berries,
    to serve

## Date Caramel

75 g/¾ cup fresh, pitted dates
    (you can also use dried dates,
    soaked for at least 2 hours,
    then drained)

1 tablespoon coconut oil

125 ml/½ cup almond milk

## Serves 2

I'm not a huge brunch person but I am partial to pancakes, and with a recipe this healthy I allow myself to indulge in them whenever I fancy. They're protein rich, so they make a great post-gym breakfast.

In a small mixing bowl, combine the almond flour, arrowroot starch, baking powder, ground cinnamon, salt and xylitol and mix well – you want to make sure the baking powder is evenly incorporated. Pour in the apple purée/applesauce, vanilla and coconut oil, then stir in half of the almond milk. Stir well, then add the remaining almond milk a little at a time, until the mixture resembles regular pancake batter. You may not need the entire amount of almond milk.

To make the date caramel, put the dates and coconut oil in a food processor and pulse until completely smooth. Pour in half of the almond milk and blend again. Add as much of the remaining almond milk as you like until the desired consistency is reached. Transfer the mixture to a small saucepan or pot and set over a low heat to warm through.

Put a small amount of coconut oil (about ½ tablespoon) in a frying pan/skillet and set over a medium–high heat. Make sure that the pan is really hot (don't skip this step) before pouring in the batter to make 2 pancakes at a time. Let the mixture sit for about 2 minutes until you see the surface start to bubble, then carefully flip the pancakes and let them warm until fully cooked through. Keep the pancakes warm while you cook the remaining batter in the same way until it is all used up. Add a little extra coconut oil to the pan each time, if necessary.

Serve the pancakes in a stack with the warm date caramel and mixed fresh berries.

**NUTRITIONAL INFORMATION**
Per serving: 180 kcals/751 kJ, 7.7 g fat (4.8 g saturated),
8.4 g protein, 16.4 g carbs (4.4 g sugars), 0.5 g salt, 4.9 g fibre

# Sweet Spreads

## Pistachio and Cacao

230 g/2 cups pistachio nuts, shelled

200 ml/³⁄₄ cup almond milk

40 g/¹⁄₄ cup cacao nibs

1 teaspoon pure vanilla extract

a pinch of salt

*a baking sheet, greased and lined with baking parchment*

## Walnut and Coconut

150 g/1¹⁄₂ cups walnuts, soaked overnight and drained

40 g/¹⁄₂ cup desiccated/ shredded coconut

3 tablespoons coconut oil

160 ml/²⁄₃ cup almond milk

4 tablespoons coconut sugar

2 teaspoons pure vanilla extract

a pinch of salt

*a baking sheet, greased and lined with baking parchment*

## Not—tella

250 g/2 cups hazelnuts, peeled

200 ml/³⁄₄ cup almond milk

50 g/heaped ¹⁄₂ cup cacao powder

100 g/¹⁄₂ cup xylitol

1 teaspoon pure vanilla extract

*a baking sheet, greased and lined with baking parchment*

## Each Makes 600 ml (20 oz.)/2¹⁄₂ cups

Like many people, I am obsessed with peanut butter. In the interest of varying my intake of nuts and seeds, I try to mix things up. Here are a few new takes on plain nut and seed butters to try. I love the Pistachio and Cacao Spread with the Coconut Yogurt on page 34 and the Not-tella Spread on the Paleo Pancakes on page 30.

Each of these spreads can be made in the same way. Preheat the oven to 180°C (350°F) Gas 4.

Spread the nuts on the prepared baking sheet and bake in the preheated oven for about 10 minutes – you want them to be slightly browned but not burned.

Remove the sheet from the oven and allow the nuts to cool completely. Put them in a food processor with the remaining ingredients and pulse until you have a smooth and creamy nut butter.

These spreads are perfect for spreading on paleo breads, lettuce leaves, celery sticks or even served as dips for vegetable sticks or seed crackers. To me, 2 tablespoons of nut butter is what I advise as a full serving of fats for a meal, and 1–1¹⁄₂ tablespoons is good as a snack.

---

**NUTRITIONAL INFORMATION**

Per serving, Pistachio and Cacao: 110 kcals/456 kJ, 8.6 g fat (1.7 g saturated), 3.6 g protein, 3.2 g carbs (1.7 g sugars), 0.1 g salt, 2.4 g fibre

Per serving, Walnut and Coconut: 136 kcals/563 kJ, 11 g fat (4.2 g saturated), 2 g protein, 6.3 g carbs (6.2 g sugars), 0.1 g salt, 1.1 g fibre

Per serving, Not-tella: 116 kcals/480 kJ, 9.1 g fat (1 g saturated), 2.9 g protein, 4.6 g carbs (0.9 g sugars), 0.1 g salt, 1.7 g fibre

---

# Coconut Yogurt with Berry Chia Jam

Good fats help balance our blood sugar levels to maintain a healthy weight. Paired with the Omega-3-rich chia jam/jelly, this coconut yogurt is true beauty food!

2 x 400-ml/14-oz. cans full-fat
  coconut milk
2 probiotic supplement capsules
  (such as Acidophilus or
  a broad-spectrum probiotic)
1 heaped teaspoon stevia,
  to sweeten
1 teaspoon lemon juice
60g/½ cup pistachio nuts,
  roughly chopped

## Berry Chia Jam/Jelly

140 g/1 cup strawberries,
  chopped
120 g/1 cup raspberries, chopped
2 teaspoons lemon juice
3 tablespoons ground chia seeds
2 teaspoons stevia

*a 14-oz. sterilized glass jar*
  *(see page 4)*

Makes 475 ml
(16 oz.)/2 cups Jam/
Jelly and Serves 2–4

Place the cans of coconut milk in the fridge for at least 8 hours, or overnight; this will solidify the healthy coconut fats and separate them from the liquid.

Once chilled, open the cans and carefully scoop off the 'cream' that has risen to the top, discarding the liquid at the bottom. Put the coconut cream in a food processor with the contents of the probiotic supplement capsules, stevia and lemon juice. Blend until well combined, then spoon the mixture into the sterilized glass jar. Carefully tap the jar on the counter to get rid of any air pockets. Wipe the jar clean and screw on the lid.

Set the sealed mixture in the oven with the light on but without actually turning the heat on for 24 hours – this ensures a warm, constant temperature that will encourage fermentation. Next, refrigerate it for 3 hours – this is when it will start to thicken.

To make the berry chia jam/jelly, place the strawberries, raspberries and lemon juice in a saucepan or pot set over medium heat. Warm through, and when the berries start to soften mash them roughly by hand using a fork or potato masher. Add the ground chia seeds and stir to combine; the mixture will thicken a little. Remove the pan from the heat, add the stevia and stir until dissolved. Cover and chill in the fridge for at least 30 minutes to allow the mixture to set. The jam/jelly can be eaten straight away or stored in a sterilized glass jar or airtight container in the fridge for up to 3–5 days.

Once the yogurt is chilled, serve in small bowls with 2 tablespoons of jam/jelly stirred through and pistachio nuts sprinkled on top. It also goes well served with granola or sliced fresh fruit. The yogurt will keep for up to 2 weeks if stored in an airtight container in the fridge.

> **NUTRITIONAL INFORMATION**
> **Per serving:** 450 kcals/1856 kJ, 43.3 g fat (36.9 g saturated),
> 3.5 g protein, 9.8 g carbs (6.8 g sugars), 0.2 g salt, 3.3 g fibre

# Eggplant 'Bacon' ELT Sandwich

Healthy breakfasts don't have to be all smoothies and baked goods –
if you like a savoury, hearty start to your day, or need a meal that'll satisfy
your hunger after a tough workout, we've got you covered.

2 avocados, peeled, pitted/
    stoned and roughly chopped
4–8 large slices raw seed bread
    (such as Lydia's Organic
    Sunflower Seed Bread)
2 large tomatoes, sliced
a handful of alfalfa sprouts
4 tablespoons olive oil

## Eggplant Bacon

1 large aubergine/eggplant
1–2 teaspoons sea salt
1 teaspoon liquid smoke
    (optional)
2 teaspoons smoked paprika
a pinch of chipotle powder
2 tablespoons olive oil
2 tablespoons balsamic vinegar

*a dehydrator (optional)*

## Makes About 20–25 Eggplant Bacon Rashers and Serves 4

Begin by preparing the eggplant bacon. If you want the recipe to
be raw, you will need a dehydrator for this recipe. If not, an oven is just
fine. Preheat the oven or dehydrator to 110°C (225°F) Gas ¼.

Using a mandoline, slice the aubergine/eggplant into very thin strips
and then cut in half lengthways so that the rashers resemble the shape
of bacon. If you don't have a mandoline, slice them by hand as thinly as
possible, bearing in mind that they needn't be neat. Place the aubergine/
eggplant strips in a casserole dish.

Mix the remaining eggplant bacon ingredients together in a small mixing
bowl with 6 tablespoons of water. Pour the mixture over the aubergine/
eggplant rashers. Set aside to soften for about 15 minutes.

Remove the aubergine/eggplant rashers from the dish and place them
on a baking sheet or dehydrator sheet, reserving the leftover marinade.
Brush the aubergine/eggplant strips lightly with the marinade, then place
in the preheated oven or dehydrator. Allow the eggplant bacon to get
really crispy – in the oven this will take 4–6 hours and in the dehydrator
it will take 16–20 hours.

To prepare the ELT sandwiches, lightly mash the avocado onto the seed
bread. Top with slices of tomato, the alfalfa sprouts and 3–4 eggplant
bacon rashers. You could top with another slice of seed bread or serve
as an open sandwich, as here. This sandwich is also delicious with a layer
of sauerkraut. Yum!

> **NUTRITIONAL INFORMATION**
> **Per serving:** 450 kcals/1861 kJ, 37 g fat (6.1 g saturated),
> 9.4 g protein, 14.3 g carbs (5.6 g sugars), 2.1 g salt, 11 g fibre

# Breakfast Crumble

Including a sizeable amount of fruit in my breakfast is one of the habits I know makes me feel really energized for the rest of the day. But, let's face it, there are some mornings when you want something a little more comforting than an ice-cold smoothie or chia pudding. Crumble is my favourite dessert on the planet, and this super-healthy version gives me the warm and cosies whilst still letting me hit my fruit quota. This would make a great after-school snack for kids, or a healthy solution for staving off those 4pm office cravings.

5 sweet red apples (try Fiji or Royal Gala), cored
110 g/$\frac{1}{2}$ cup coconut sugar
220 g/2 cups almond flour
1 teaspoon ground cinnamon
$\frac{1}{2}$ teaspoon ground nutmeg
$\frac{1}{2}$ teaspoon ground cloves
1 teaspoon salt
160 ml/$\frac{2}{3}$ cup coconut oil, melted
2 teaspoons pure vanilla extract
Coconut Yogurt (see page 34), to serve

SERVES 4

Preheat the oven to 180°C (350°F) Gas 4.

Slice the apples into pieces about 2$\frac{1}{2}$ cm/1 inch thick and spread them on the bottom of a baking dish. Scatter about 4 tablespoons of the coconut sugar on top and toss to coat the apples well.

Put the almond flour, spices, salt and remaining coconut sugar in a large mixing bowl and stir to combine. Stir in the coconut oil and vanilla. Spread the crumble mixture evenly over the apples in the baking dish – it doesn't have to be neat and I tend to use my hands to do this.

Cover the dish with foil and bake in the preheated oven for 50 minutes. Remove the foil and bake for another 10 minutes, or until the topping has browned.

Serve immediately with Coconut Yogurt on the side.

---

**NUTRITIONAL INFORMATION**
**Per serving:** 620 kcals/2583 kJ, 35.6 g fat (26 g saturated), 22.7 g protein, 43.9 g carbs (42.8 g sugars), 1.3 g salt, 14 g fibre

---

# PUNCHY MUNCHIES

Most often when I eat something I wish I hadn't, it's because I was tired or hungry, or grumpy, and didn't have access to something healthy. At that point I'm weak-willed and out of discipline, so I resort to something sugary and refined, even though I know it won't help fix anything. This is where punchy munchies come in – my arsenal of good-mood-food guarantees to give me a boost whenever my day calls for it.

## Curried Sweet Potato

2 medium sweet potatoes

5 tablespoons coconut oil

1 tablespoon curry powder

## Brussels Sprouts

400g/4 cups Brussels sprouts

1 tablespoon olive oil (or freshly
squeezed lime juice)

½ tablespoon ground cumin

½ teaspoon salt

## Beetroot/Beet

2 beetroots/beets, peeled

1 golden beetroot/beet, peeled

1 tablespoon olive oil

sea salt, to serve

*1–2 baking sheets, greased and
lined with baking parchment*

## Each Serves 4

---

NUTRITIONAL
INFORMATION

Per serving,
Curried Sweet Potato:
206 kcals/857 kJ, 14.2 g fat
(12 g saturated), 1.2 g protein,
16.8 g carbs (4.4 g sugars),
0.1 g salt, 3.3 g fibre

*For Brussels Sprouts
and Beetroot/Beet Crisps,
see page 141*

---

# Curried Sweet Potato

Preheat your oven to 200°C (400°F) Gas 6.

Thinly slice the sweet potatoes into rounds using either a peeler or mandoline and place them in a large shallow dish.

Warm the coconut oil in a small saucepan or pot set over a low heat until liquefied. Remove from the heat and stir in the curry powder. Pour the heated mixture over the sweet potato rounds, carefully toss to coat the vegetable slices, then remove the rounds and place them on the prepared baking sheets.

Bake in the preheated oven for 22 minutes, or until completely crisp – check them halfway through cooking and turn over if necessary. Remove from the oven and serve in bowls.

# Brussels Sprouts

Preheat your oven to 180°C (350°F) Gas 4.

Using a sharp knife, carefully slice off the very bottom of the Brussels sprouts to render the leaves loose. Remove as many leaves as you can until you're just left with the core, discarding the cores.

Put the leaves in a large mixing bowl and toss in the olive oil, cumin and salt. For an oil-free option, you can substitute lime juice for the olive oil.

Arrange the leaves on the prepared baking sheet and bake in the preheated oven for 10–12 minutes, until the leaves are crispy and dry. Remove from the oven and serve in bowls.

# Beetroot/Beet

Preheat your oven to 180°C (350°F) Gas 4.

Using a sharp knife, thinly slice off the very bottoms and tops of the beetroots/beets and golden beetroot/beet. Thinly slice the trimmed beetroots/beets into rounds using either a peeler or mandoline and place them in a large shallow dish.

Toss in the olive oil to coat, transfer to the prepared baking sheet and bake in the preheated oven for 20–22 minutes, or until nicely crisped up.

Remove from the oven and drain on paper towels to remove any excess oil. Sprinkle with sea salt and serve.

# CRAVEABLE CRISPS

There's a certain satisfaction that only a salty, crunchy crisp/chip can give you.
I get frustrated when I see diet swaps that recommend swapping crisps for
something like sticks of celery because usually what happens is that we eat
the celery, feel unsatisfied, then end up eating the crisps/chips later anyway.
I think these veggie crisps/chips do a pretty darn good job as stand-ins.

Sweet potato and fries are having their moment in the spotlight. These 'fries' have the benefit of being baked rather than fried, which not only reduces the calorie count but also cuts out the carcinogenic trans-fats that the frying process creates.

# Chilli-cheese Butternut Squash Fries

1 medium butternut squash, peeled
1 small red chilli/chile
4 tablespoons cashew butter
1 tablespoon olive oil
1 teaspoon salt
2 tablespoons nutritional yeast

sweet and spicy sauce (try Frank's hot sauce), to serve

*a baking sheet, greased and lined with baking parchment*

SERVES 4

Preheat the oven to 220°C (425°F) Gas 7.

Slice the butternut squash into thick batons and set aside.

Thinly slice the red chilli/chile into small pieces, discarding the seeds (unless you want the fries super spicy!), and mix together with the cashew butter, olive oil and salt in a large mixing bowl.

Add the fries to the mixture and toss to coat, then dip each one in the nutritional yeast. Transfer to the prepared baking sheet and bake in the preheated oven for 40 minutes, turning halfway through cooking.

Remove from the oven and serve with sweet and spicy sauce.

# Baked Jicama Fries

1 jicama/water chestnut
1½ teaspoons paprika
½ teaspoon garlic powder
1 teaspoon onion powder
¾ teaspoon salt

chimichurri sauce, to serve

*a baking sheet, greased and lined with baking parchment*

SERVES 2

Preheat the oven to 180°C (350°F) Gas 4.

Peel the jicama and slice it into thin matchsticks. The jicama will be quite moist, so pat the sticks dry between paper towels.

Once dry, put the jicama sticks in a large mixing bowl, add the seasonings and toss to coat.

Transfer the fries to the prepared baking sheet and bake in the preheated oven for 1 hour 10 minutes.

Remove from the oven and serve with chimichurri sauce.

---

NUTRITIONAL INFORMATION

Per serving, Chilli-cheese Butternut Squash Fries: 252 kcals/1053 kJ, 11.3 g fat (2.2 g saturated), 9.1 g protein, 25 g carbs (10.9 g sugars), 1.5 g salt, 7.2 g fibre

*For Baked Jicama Fries, see page 141*

# Hot Spinach and Artichoke Dip

I love the taste of this dip and find it's one of those things that once you start eating it, you just can't stop. With this version there's no reason to stop – it's all good stuff – so enjoy!

1 x 390-g/14-oz. can artichokes

30 g/ ¾ cup macadamia nuts

200 ml/ ¾ cup non-dairy milk (such as almond, soy, or coconut milk)

½ tablespoon salt

2 garlic cloves

3 tablespoons nutritional yeast

½ white onion, diced

olive oil, for sautéing

½ tablespoon arrowroot starch

400 g/8 cups spinach

chilli/hot pepper flakes (optional)

crudités, to serve

*a high-speed blender*

*6 ceramic ramekins*

## Serves 6

Preheat your oven to 200°C (400°F) Gas 6.

Cut the artichokes into small bite-sized pieces and set aside.

Put the macadamia nuts, non-dairy milk, salt, garlic and nutritional yeast in a high-speed blender and blend until completely smooth.

Sauté the onions in a little olive oil in a large frying pan/skillet set over a medium heat. Once browned, pour in the macadamia nut mixture and stir in the arrowroot. The mixture will start to thicken.

Divide the spinach and artichokes between your ramekins and pour some of the warm macadamia mixture over the vegetables. Sprinkle each ramekin with chilli/hot pepper flakes, if using.

Place the filled ramekins on a baking sheet and bake in the preheated oven for about 18 minutes, or until the tops have hardened.

Serve immediately with your choice of crudités. These are best eaten warm but can be kept for up to 4 days in the fridge.

### Top Tip

I also love to make a main meal using this recipe by serving one ramekin with a bowl of warm quinoa and cooked veggies.

---

**NUTRITIONAL INFORMATION**
Per serving: 120 kcals/499 kJ, 5.9 g fat (1.1 g saturated), 8 g protein, 6 g carbs (2.5 g sugars), 2 g salt, 5.3 g fibre

---

# Cauli-pops

I love pre-dinner noshing, especially if it's also social. However, it's so easy to over-do it on puff pastry creations and little blinis, then feel too full for the main event. These cauli-pops are just enough to take the edge off, without being too heavy.

1 large head cauliflower, roughly chopped
100 g/½ cup nutritional yeast
3 heaped tablespoons almond flour
1 garlic clove
½ tablespoon onion powder
½ tablespoon dried thyme
freshly ground black pepper
vegetable oil, for frying
za'atar, to coat
a baking sheet, greased

SERVES 8

Boil the cauliflower until soft in a pan of water set over medium heat. Once cooked, drain using a colander and pat dry with paper towels.

Put the cooked cauliflower in a food processor and add the remaining ingredients. Pulse until smooth.

Roll large teaspoonfuls of the cauliflower mixture into balls and place on the prepared baking sheet.

Fill a large frying pan/skillet with vegetable oil so it is 2½ cm/1 inch deep. Set over a medium–high heat and, when hot, drop a small amount of the cauliflower batter into the pan – if it sizzles, the oil is ready to cook with. Carefully put the cauliflower balls into the pan and cook for 2–3 minutes on each side.

Remove the cauli-pops with a slotted spoon and drain on paper towels.

Once cooked, spear the cauli-pops with toothpicks and roll in za'atar spice mix if desired, then serve immediately.

## Top Tip

Any leftover cauli-pops can be stored in an airtight container and eaten the next day – try mashing them into a bowl and top with some protein for a comforting dinner.

---

### NUTRITIONAL INFORMATION
**Per serving:** 85 kcals/355 kJ, 1.8 g fat (0.5 g saturated), 10.3 g protein, 4.2 g carbs (2 g sugars), 0.3 g salt, 5.2 g fibre

# Almond-Crusted Buffalo Bites with Cashew Mayo

I love the social aspect of food and how it brings people together, especially for larger shared events, like Christmas, Thanksgiving and Halloween. This one makes me think of the Superbowl, a night when 1¼ billion buffalo chicken wings are consumed. I'm not against the occasional junk-y treat, but if there's a way that you can indulge your cravings more often, and in a kinder way to your body, why not?

85 g/¾ cup coconut flour

30 g/¼ cup almond meal (or use more coconut flour)

1 teaspoon garlic powder

1½ teaspoons onion powder

½ teaspoon salt

1 large head of cauliflower, cut into florets

1 tablespoon olive oil

150 ml/⅔ cup sugar-free hot sauce (I like Frank's RedHot)

## Cashew Mayo

120 g/1 cup cashew nuts, soaked for 2 hours and drained

2 tablespoons freshly squeezed lemon juice

2 tablespoons apple cider vinegar

¾ teaspoon sea salt

1 teaspoon honey (or use agave or maple syrup)

*a baking sheet, greased and lined with baking parchment*

## Serves 8

Preheat the oven to 220°C (425°F) Gas 7.

In a large mixing bowl, combine the coconut flour, almond meal, if using, garlic and onion powders and salt with 250 ml/1 cup of water.

Dip each cauliflower floret individually into the mixture so that it's fully coated. Place them on the prepared baking sheet and bake in the preheated oven for 15 minutes. Meanwhile, whisk the olive oil and hot sauce together in a bowl.

Remove the cauliflower from the oven and dip each floret in the hot sauce mixture, making sure they are well coated. Return to the oven for another 20 minutes.

To make the cashew mayo, place the cashews, lemon juice, cider vinegar, sea salt and honey (or agave or maple syrup) in a food processor and blend until smooth. With the motor running, drizzle in 4–6 tablespoons of water, one at a time, until you have a thick dipping consistency.

Serve the baked cauliflower with the cashew mayo as an appetizer, snack or as a side dish for a main course.

## Top Tip

These buffalo bites work really well with the Chilli Rellenos on page 111.

> **NUTRITIONAL INFORMATION**
> **Per serving:** (if using honey) 251 kcals/1043 kJ, 15.3 g fat (4.4 g saturated), 12.3 g protein, 11.3 g carbs (5.6 g sugars), 2.1 g salt, 9.4 g fibre

## Cocoa Coconut

40 g/½ cup desiccated/shredded coconut

30 g/¼ cup cocoa powder, plus extra for rolling

3 tablespoons sugar-free honey (or use agave or maple syrup)

2 teaspoons granulated stevia

3 tablespoons coconut oil

1½ teaspoons pure vanilla extract

## Winter Spice

40 g/½ cup desiccated/shredded coconut, plus extra for rolling

30 g/¼ cup almond meal

4 tablespoons sugar-free blackstrap molasses

1 teaspoon granulated stevia

½ teaspoon grated fresh or ground ginger

½ teaspoon ground cinnamon

¼ teaspoon ground nutmeg

3 tablespoons coconut oil

## Apple and Cinnamon

40 g/½ cup desiccated/shredded coconut, plus extra for rolling

30 g/¼ almond meal

4 tablespoons sugar-free apple purée (or applesauce)

¾ teaspoons ground cinnamon

1 teaspoon granulated stevia

1 teaspoon pure vanilla extract

3 tablespoons coconut oil

## Each Makes 8–10

# Hand-rolled Macaroons

These were the first raw dessert I learned to make, and they're the easiest, too. They are the perfect mid-morning munchy as well as a great sweet ending to a meal when you just want a few bites of something sweet, rather than a full-on dessert.

Each of these macaroons can be made in the same way. Put all of the ingredients into a mixing bowl and stir to combine.

Shape the mixture into balls using your hands or a melon baller, arrange on a clean baking sheet and transfer to the fridge to chill for at least 20 minutes, or until firm.

Meanwhile, sift a little extra cocoa powder onto a wide plate and set aside.

Remove the macaroons from the fridge and roll them in the cocoa powder before serving.

## Variations

For a variation, try rolling the Winter Spice macaroons and Apple and Cinnamon macaroons in desiccated/shredded coconut, instead of cocoa powder.

### NUTRITIONAL INFORMATION

Per macaroon, Cocoa Coconut Macaroons: (if using honey) 113 kcals/468 kJ, 8.1 g fat (12.7 g saturated), 1.3 g protein, 7.7 g carbs (7.3 g sugars), 0.1 g salt, 1.5 g fibre

*For Winter Spice and Apple and Cinnamon Macaroons, see page 141*

# Protein Truffles

A lot of energy-bite snacks use either oats or dried fruit as a base, but what if you want to avoid both? If you're simply looking for a quick way to eat a good protein and fat combo that isn't a rolled-up turkey slice, power up with these truffles. And don't let their cuteness fool you – they taste like dessert but keep you trim.

2 scoops protein powder
  (see page 4 for information
  on serving sizes)
3 tablespoons coconut flour
¾ tablespoon granulated stevia
3 tablespoons coconut oil
2 tablespoons tahini
½ teaspoon pure vanilla extract

*a 12-hole heart-shaped
  chocolate mould or silicone
  ice tray (optional)*

Makes 12

Put the protein powder, coconut flour and stevia in a large mixing bowl and stir to combine.

If your coconut oil is solid, gently melt it in a saucepan or pot set over a medium heat until liquefied.

Pour the melted coconut oil, tahini and vanilla into the dry mixture and stir well.

Scoop the batter into the mould or roll into small balls. Cover and put in the fridge to chill for at least 20 minutes, or until firm.

Turn out the truffles from the mould and enjoy.

---

**NUTRITIONAL INFORMATION**
**Per truffle:** 72 kcals/298 kJ, 5.2 g fat (3 g saturated), 4.5 g protein, 0.8 g carbs (0.2 g sugars), 0.1 g salt, 1.7 g fibre

---

# SUPER SALADS AND SIDES

These aren't wimpy salads. Think of a salad as a vehicle for any craving you might have: create a base of greens and just add in anything that sounds good to you at the time. There is no such thing as a bad combination. Take the recipes on the following pages as starting points for infinite delicious creations of your own.

# Ume Carpaccio

If you're having people over and wondering what to make, this is the dish to serve. Umeboshi paste is an unusual ingredient that's really delicious and it makes a nice change from the usual dressing staples we overly rely on. Switching things up just by using different condiments is an easy way to ensure you don't get tired of eating well.

35 g/¼ cup pumpkin seeds
12 asparagus spears
12 radishes (or 2 large watermelon radishes)
2 large handfuls of rocket/ arugula
80 g/2 cups mixed micro greens, such as micro chives

## Umeboshi Dressing
6 tablespoons umeboshi paste
100 ml/⅓ cup mirin
60 ml/¼ cup toasted sesame oil
freshly ground black pepper

## Serves 4

Begin by toasting the pumpkin seeds in a dry frying pan/skillet set over a medium heat until brown. Remove from the heat and set aside.

Chop the asparagus into about 7½-cm/3-inch pieces and toss into a metal colander. Bring a pot of water to the boil over a medium–high heat and place the colander on top, taking care not to let the base of the colander touch the water. Reduce the heat, cover and steam the asparagus for 6–7 minutes, until the asparagus is tender but not too soft. Transfer to a small plate and set aside to cool.

Meanwhile, thinly slice the radishes using a mandoline or vegetable peeler.

To make the umeboshi dressing, put the umeboshi paste, mirin and sesame oil in a small mixing bowl and mix well. Season with black pepper.

Arrange the radishes on a serving plate, place the cooled asparagus on top and scatter with rocket/arugula. Top with the micro greens, then pour the umeboshi dressing over the whole dish and sprinkle with the toasted pumpkin seeds.

### NUTRITIONAL INFORMATION
Per serving: 274 kcals/1141 kJ, 15.9 g fat (2.3 g saturated), 6.2 g protein, 23.9 g carbs (13.1 g sugars), 4.4 g salt, 5.2 g fibre

# Asian Kale Salad

This is the salad I make most often. It's packed with so many different flavours that each bite tastes different. I've converted many kale-weary people into fans with it – the trick is to massage the kale thoroughly so that it becomes soft and more palatable. This salad keeps so well that it's best to make a big batch for convenience. If it's in my fridge, I'll often eat it for breakfast or lunch, or dinner. Whenever!

1 large head of curly kale (or cavolo nero)

3–4 tablespoons black truffle oil

1 teaspoon pink Himalayan salt (or sea salt)

2 carrots

1/2 large cucumber

a sprig each of fresh mint, flat-leaf parsley and coriander/cilantro, roughly chopped

4 spring onions/scallions, chopped

freshly squeezed juice of 2 limes

1 tablespoon Bragg liquid aminos (or substitute)

3 tablespoons nutritional yeast

3 tablespoons hemp seeds

1 avocado, peeled, stoned/pitted and cut into cubes

*a spiralizer (optional)*

SERVES 4 AS A MAIN
OR 6 AS AN APPETIZER

Tear the kale leaves into pieces and wash them in a sieve/strainer under cold running water. Pat the leaves dry with paper towels and, once dry, put them in a large salad bowl.

Add the black truffle oil and Himalayan salt to the bowl, then, using your hands, massage the kale until the fibres soften up and the oil evenly coats the leaves.

Next, prepare the carrots and cucumber by slicing them using a spiralizer. Alternatively, slice them very thinly lengthways with a sharp knife.

Add the carrots, cucumber, fresh herbs and spring onions/scallions to the salad bowl, along with the lime juice.

Toss all the ingredients together, then add the liquid aminos, nutritional yeast, hemp seeds and avocado pieces before serving.

### NUTRITIONAL INFORMATION
Per serving: 282 kcals/1168 kJ, 20.6 g fat (3.5 g saturated), 11.3 g protein, 8.7 g carbs (5.2 g sugars), 2.1 g salt, 8.6 g fibre

# Spicy Green Papaya Salad

I'm a spicy food addict. It doesn't sound so unhealthy, but when you consider that most spicy condiments are loaded with salt (and I use them liberally), it adds up to excessive sodium consumption – cue water retention, facial puffiness and an unhappy mineral balance inside. The simple solution: try to use fresh chillies/chiles for a lighter dish that is a refreshing way to get a spice fix.

1 young green papaya
2 carrots
1 garlic clove
1 Thai red chilli/chile
   (or jalapeño)
3 plum tomatoes, halved
220 g/1¾ cups green beans
90 g/¾ cup cashew nuts
a bunch of fresh
   coriander/cilantro
freshly squeezed juice of 2 limes
2 tablespoons soy sauce
1 tablespoon granulated stevia

SERVES 2

Shred the green papaya and pat dry using paper towels. Transfer to a large mixing bowl and grate in the carrot. Mix and set aside.

Crush the garlic and Thai red chilli/chile using a pestle and mortar (or you can achieve the same effect by using the bottom of a rolling pin and a chopping board). Add the tomatoes and the green beans and crush lightly – you want the tomatoes to be bruised and the green beans to be soft.

Toast the cashew nuts in a dry frying pan/skillet set over a medium heat until golden.

Put 60 g/½ cup of the toasted cashew nuts in a food processor and pulse to a crumb. Transfer to the bowl with the papaya and carrot in. Add the crushed tomato and green bean mixture, and the coriander/cilantro. Add the lime juice, soy sauce and stevia and toss everything together.

Divide the salad between 2 serving dishes and top with the remaining whole toasted cashews.

# Raw Mexican Salad

1 head Romaine lettuce, chopped
1 yellow pepper, diced
300 g/2 cups cherry tomatoes, chopped
2 small handfuls of alfalfa sprouts
¼ red onion, diced (optional)

## Tomato-Mango Salsa
2 large tomatoes
150 g/1 cup cherry tomatoes
¼ red onion, diced
1 mango, peeled, stoned/pitted and chopped
2 tablespoons extra virgin olive oil
freshly squeezed juice of ½ lemon

## Artichoke 'Meat'
250 g/2½ cups artichoke hearts
3 tablespoons extra virgin olive oil
1 garlic clove, crushed
a few sprigs of fresh flat-leaf parsley
freshly squeezed juice of ½ lemon

## Guacamole
3 avocados, peeled, stoned/pitted and roughly chopped
freshly squeezed juice of 2 limes
¼ red onion, diced
a bunch of fresh coriander/cilantro

*a high-speed blender*

## Serves 2

I love salads with lots of different components to them. An easy way to come up with combinations is to think of different cuisines and the flavours that they're known for. This salad features all the common flavours in Mexican food: salsa, onions, peppers, guacamole and a meaty pâté provided by the artichoke. What's more, this recipe is totally raw if made with extra virgin olive oil, which is cold-pressed.

Begin by making the tomato-mango salsa. Put the tomatoes, red onion and mango in a blender. With the motor running, drizzle in the olive oil and lemon juice.

To make the artichoke meat, pulse all of the ingredients together in a food processor, until very smooth.

To make the guacamole, place the flesh of the avocados in a bowl with the rest of the ingredients and mash together with a fork until well combined but still chunky.

To serve, divide the lettuce, yellow pepper, tomatoes, alfalfa sprouts and red onion (if using) between two large bowls. Top each salad with a generous portion of the salsa, the guacamole and the artichoke meat.

### Note
If you are trying a raw vegan diet but want to keep some animal protein, you could replace the artichoke meat with a simple tuna ceviche. Combine finely diced tuna or yellowtail with lots of lemon and lime juice, some coriander/cilantro, chopped spring onions/scallions and a dash of coconut milk.

---

**NUTRITIONAL INFORMATION**
Per serving: 963 kcals/3988 kJ, 74.2 g fat (13.8 g saturated), 18 g protein, 42.6 g carbs (36 g sugars), 0.3 g salt, 26.6 g fibre

# Evergreen Salad

The main alkaline minerals are calcium, magnesium, potassium and sodium, and this salad is bursting with all four! Add to that pak choi/bok choy and tahini, two of the top-most absorbable calcium food sources, and you'll have a salad that's good for kicking a dairy habit.

1 orange
2 lemons
200 g/2 cups baby pak choi/bok choy
    leaves, roughly chopped
120 g/3 cups Baby Gem (or other pale
    green) lettuce, roughly chopped
the leaves of 2–3 stalks of fresh mint,
    coriander/cilantro, and Thai basil

1 bulb fennel, finely sliced
2 teaspoons sesame seeds, to serve

### Tahini Dressing
4 tablespoons tahini
2 teaspoons grated fresh ginger

### Serves 2

Begin by grating the zest of the orange and lemons and set aside.

For the base of the salad, put the chopped pak choi/bok choy and lettuce in a large mixing bowl with the herbs. Add the sliced fennel and toss to combine.

Peel the orange and divide into sections. Add to the salad, mix and set aside.

To make the dressing, squeeze the juice from the lemons. Stir together the lemon juice, tahini, reserved zest of the orange and lemons, grated ginger and 3–4 tablespoons of water.

Pour the dressing over the salad and mix through (I like to use my hands to do this). Top with the sesame seeds and serve.

> **NUTRITIONAL INFORMATION**
> Per serving: 360 kcals/1491 kJ, 25.6 g fat (3.7 g saturated), 13.6 g protein, 12.4 g carbs (11.3 g sugars), 0.2 g salt, 13 g fibre

# WALDORF SALAD

This salad, named after the hotel where it was invented in 1896, feels very elegant. Where the original was made with generous amounts of mayonnaise, I've used an avocado-based dressing to sneak in extra nutrition.

50 g/$\frac{1}{2}$ cup walnuts
1 head butterhead lettuce
$\frac{1}{2}$ head radicchio
3 sticks celery, sliced
225 g/1$\frac{1}{2}$ cups red grapes, halved
1 green apple, cored and sliced

## WALDORF DRESSING

1 avocado, peeled, stoned/pitted and roughly chopped
1 teaspoon English mustard
2 tablespoons white wine vinegar

## SERVES 2

Begin by toasting the walnuts in a dry frying pan/skillet set over a medium heat until they are crispy and browned. Remove from the heat and set aside (it's ok if you nibble on a few while you prepare the rest of the meal though!).

Tear off the larger leaves from the head of butterhead lettuce and layer them on the bottom of your plates or serving dish.

Chop the rest of the lettuce along with the radicchio and put it in a large mixing bowl. Add the sliced celery, grapes, apple and toasted walnuts.

To make the Waldorf dressing, mash the avocado in a small mixing bowl. Add the mustard and white wine vinegar and whisk to combine. Add 1–2 tablespoons of water to thin out the mixture, then add to the mixed salad. Toss until everything is well coated, then spoon the mixture onto the large butterhead lettuce leaves on your serving plates.

NUTRITIONAL INFORMATION
Per serving: 461 kcals/1914 kJ, 32.6 g fat (5 g saturated), 9 g protein, 27.6 g carbs (26.3 g sugars), 0.4 g salt, 11.1 g fibre

# Kale Caesar

Caesar salad is one of the most popular salads in the world; here it is with a healthy makeover. Nutrient-dense kale replaces the iceberg lettuce, the almonds and nutritional yeast stand in for the cream and cheese, and the salty hit is provided by nori seaweed. I also use cucumber in this salad, because I think it's a nice contrast to all the other strong flavours.

1 large bunch of kale
½ teaspoon salt
1 tablespoon olive oil
10-cm/4-inch piece of cucumber, sliced
2 large nori sheets
1–2 seed crackers, roughly chopped

## Miso Dressing

2 tablespoons white miso
2 teaspoons capers
1 tablespoon nutritional yeast
freshly squeezed juice of ½ lemon
60 g/¼ cup your choice of nuts (brazil nuts, almonds, macadamia nuts), soaked overnight and drained

*a high-speed blender*

## Serves 2

Tear the kale into rough pieces, discarding the stems. Put the kale in a large salad bowl with the salt and olive oil, and, using your hands, massage the kale until it softens. Add the cucumber slices to the bowl and set aside.

To make the miso dressing, put all of the ingredients in a blender with 2 tablespoons of water and blend until completely smooth.

Pour the dressing over the kale salad, tear in the nori sheets and scatter over the roughly chopped seed crackers.

Serve immediately, or I also love to eat this salad when it's day-old and the flavours have really developed.

NUTRITIONAL INFORMATION
Per serving: 412 kcals/1709 kJ, 26.9 g fat (2.6 g saturated), 19.8 g protein, 16.7 g carbs (4.5 g sugars), 3.5 g salt, 12 g fibre

# CAULIFLOWER RICE TWO WAYS

Who knew that when you're craving rice but don't want the heavy feeling it can sometimes give us, you can substitute it by blitzing a bit of humble cauliflower in your food processor? From there, you can use it as a substitute in any and every rice dish you like. Below are two of my favourite uses, but you'll also find it in the Raw Sushi on page 82.

1 large head cauliflower
1 tablespoon ground cumin
1 tablespoon curry powder
1 teaspoon ground turmeric
1 tablespoon grated lemon zest
2 tablespoons freshly squeezed
   lemon juice
1 teaspoon salt
1 tablespoon olive oil
4 tablespoons ground almonds
2 tablespoons (dark) raisins
2 tablespoons dried cranberries
2 tablespoons cashew nuts
2 tablespoons flaked/slivered
   almonds, to serve
10 g/¼ cup fresh flat-leaf parsley,
   finely chopped, to serve

SERVES 4

# Couscous

Begin by blending the cauliflower in a food processor to a fine rice-like texture. 1 large head of cauliflower should yield about 600 g/2 cups cauliflower rice.

Put the cauliflower rice, cumin, curry powder, turmeric, lemon zest, lemon juice, salt and olive oil in a large mixing bowl. Stir until the spices are well incorporated and the rice begins to look yellow. Add the ground almonds, raisins, cranberries and cashew nuts and stir again.

To serve, sprinkle with flaked/slivered almonds and flat-leaf parsley, and drizzle with a little extra olive oil, if desired.

> NUTRITIONAL INFORMATION
> Per serving: 312 kcals/1305 kJ, 15.9 g fat (1.9 g saturated),
> 11.3 g protein, 28.2 g carbs (24.2 g sugars), 1.4 g salt, 5.8 g fibre

1 medium head cauliflower
2 tablespoons pumpkin seeds
2 tablespoons toasted sesame oil
2 tablespoons nama shoyu (or
   tamari soy sauce or Bragg
   liquid aminos)
½ courgette/zucchini, diced
¼ white onion, finely chopped
2 carrots, finely chopped
1 garlic clove, crushed
2 spring onions/scallions, finely
   sliced, to serve

SERVES 2

# Fried Rice

Prepare the cauliflower rice as above. You need about 400 g/1½ cups.

Put the pumpkin seeds in a dry frying pan/skillet set over a medium heat and toast until browned. Transfer to a bowl and set aside.

To the same pan, add the sesame oil, nama shoyu, courgette/zucchini and onion, and sauté until the onions have browned. Add the carrots, garlic and cauliflower rice and stir-fry until the cauliflower rice has softened (about 4–5 minutes). Remove from the heat and divide between bowls, topping each with half the toasted pumpkin seeds and spring onions/scallions.

> NUTRITIONAL INFORMATION
> Per serving: 338 kcals/1405 kJ, 20.6 g fat (3.3 g saturated),
> 15.5 g protein, 17.8 g carbs (13 g sugars), 1.7 g salt, 10 g fibre

# SAUER-CARROT

I'm a true believer that a healthy gut is central to good health. There's a lot of talk about the importance of taking probiotic supplements, but for a homemade alternative try fermented foods. You can ferment almost any vegetable combination you wish. This is my version of sauerkraut, usually made using shredded cabbage. Radishes, cucumbers and beetroots/beets also work well. You can boost your immune system and ease all kinds of digestive problems by adding a scoop of fermented foods to one meal daily.

550 g/4 cups shredded carrot
2½-cm/1-inch piece of fresh
   ginger, grated
3 tablespoons dulse or nori
   seaweed flakes (optional)
2½ tablespoons salt
2 probiotic supplement capsules
   (such as Acidophilus or
   a broad-spectrum probiotic)
4–5 outer leaves from a cabbage

*a large wide-mouth, sterilized
   glass jar*

SERVES 6

Put the shredded carrot, grated ginger, seaweed flakes (if using), salt and the contents of the probiotic capsules in a large mixing bowl. Mix well by hand and set aside.

Line the glass jar with cabbage leaves, then fill with the carrot mixture, pressing it down as you go. Fill the jar to about 5 cm/2 inches from the top. Pour in enough water to cover the mixture completely, then cover it with one more cabbage leaf.

Screw the lid loosely on the jar – you don't want it to be airtight as it will negatively affect the fermentation process.

Place the jar in a warm environment (about 22°C/72°F) to ferment. In the summer, this should take about 3 days, but in winter it could take 7–9 days. To help the process along, you can wrap the jar in a dry kitchen cloth or place it in the oven with just the light on.

The way to tell if your mixture is done fermenting is to open it and taste the sauer-carrot for tanginess.

> NUTRITIONAL INFORMATION
> **Per serving:** 51 kcals/215 kJ, 0.4 g fat (0.1 g saturated),
> 1.5 g protein, 8.1 g carbs (7.5 g sugars), 2.2 g salt, 4.7 g fibre

# LIGHT LUNCHES

A light lunch doesn't have to be a depriving one – in fact, if you skimp on nutrition midday, you're more likely to feel that slump later on. To me, a light lunch isn't cutting calories or 'saving up' for later; it's keeping things simple and easy for your digestion in order to feel light and energized. Give your tank a top-up that won't weigh it down with a lunch that is a little pause to look forward to in your day.

# Green Energy Soup

Fresh soups are the ultimate light lunch and a super-healthy option. Store-bought varieties are often loaded with cream, excessive amounts of salt, and inevitably, tonnes of preservatives in order for them to survive on the shelf, so avoid them if you can. If you love soup and want all the benefits of the easy-to-assimilate nutrients, whizzing this up at home will take less time than it takes to run out and buy one. Soups are usually too low in calories to qualify as a lunch on their own, so consume it with a side of root vegetables or protein to avoid sugar cravings later on in the day.

3 kale leaves, de-stalked

a 15-cm/6-inch piece of
    cucumber

½ red (bell) pepper

1 teaspoon grated fresh ginger

freshly squeezed juice of 1 lemon

1 avocado, peeled, stoned/pitted

250 ml/1 cup coconut water

1 medium tomato, halved

4 tablespoons chopped fresh dill,
    plus extra to serve

1 garlic clove

¼ onion

½ teaspoon salt

freshly ground black pepper,
    to serve

olive oil, to serve

*a high-speed blender*

SERVES 2

Put all of the ingredients in a blender and blitz on a low speed until completely smooth.

Transfer the mixture to a small saucepan or pot set over a medium heat and warm through.

Pour into serving bowls, drizzle with olive oil, sprinkle with black pepper and a few extra sprigs of dill, and serve immediately.

NUTRITIONAL INFORMATION
Per serving: 255 kcals/1058 kJ, 17.3 g fat (3.6 g saturated), 5.6 g protein, 15.2 g carbs (13.2 g sugars), 1.7 g salt, 8.2 g fibre

# Cauliflower Pizzettas

Often, the hardest part about changing your diet is the idea of change itself. My best tip for embracing change is to make it seem like there isn't any change going on at all. So instead of saying 'I'm giving up pizza', say 'I'm going to eat pizzettas for lunch!'

3 tablespoons ground chia seeds
600 g/2 cups cauliflower rice
(see page 73)
55 g/½ cup ground almonds
½ teaspoon dried oregano
½ teaspoon dried rosemary
½ teaspoon dried basil
½ teaspoon herb salt (or salt)
½ teaspoon baking powder
1 tablespoon psyllium husk
powder

## Toppings
150 g/¾ cup ready-made tomato
pasta sauce
100 g/1 cup grilled/broiled
aubergine/eggplant
80 g/1 cup chargrilled artichokes
6–8 cherry tomatoes
a bunch of fresh basil
*a baking sheet, greased and
lined with baking parchment*

## Makes 4

For the cauliflower base, first mix the ground chia seeds with 135 ml/ generous ½ cup of water in a small mixing bowl. Whisk lightly with a fork until well combined and put in the fridge to set.

Bring a pan of water to the boil over a medium–high heat. Add the cauliflower rice, reduce the heat and cook for 7–8 minutes, until it softens. Strain the cooked cauliflower using a fine mesh sieve/strainer to remove as much water as possible, then set aside to cool completely. Drain again by pressing the cauliflower with the back of a wooden spoon.

Preheat the oven to 200°C (400°F) Gas 6.

Put the cauliflower in a large mixing bowl with the ground almonds, dried herbs, salt and baking powder. Add the chilled chia mixture, which should be gloopy and thick, and mix well using your hands to ensure the chia is well spread throughout the dough. Add the psyllium husk powder, mix, cover and set aside for 30–45 minutes.

Cut the dough into four pieces and shape it into rounds by hand, each about 7½ cm/3 inches wide and 13 mm/½ inch thick. Place on the prepared baking sheet and bake in the preheated oven for 30 minutes. Remove from the oven, turn the pizzettas over onto a clean sheet of baking parchment, transfer to the baking sheet and bake again for another 15 minutes.

Remove the bases from the oven and reduce the heat to 150°C (300°F) Gas 2. Spread each base with tomato pasta sauce and add the toppings. Return the pizzettas to the oven for a final 5 minutes.

Remove from the oven, scatter with fresh basil and serve hot.

---

**NUTRITIONAL INFORMATION**
**Per pizzetta:** 247 kcals/1024 kJ, 15 g fat (1.7 g saturated), 12 g protein, 10.1 g carbs (7.2 g sugars), 1.1 g salt, 11.9 g fibre

# Raw Sushi

This is a great way of using cauliflower rice. It doesn't hold together as well as regular rice does, so if you're new to the technique, try making the sushi rolls with it first, before the more complicated hand rolls.

300 g/1 cup cauliflower rice (see page 73)

1½ tablespoons rice vinegar (or brown rice vinegar)

1 tablespoon nama shoyu (raw soy sauce, tamari soy sauce, or Bragg's liquid aminos)

1 teaspoon freshly squeezed lemon juice

10 x 20-cm/8-inch square nori sheets

1 red (bell) pepper, finely sliced

2 spring onions/scallions

60 g/1 cup enoki mushrooms

1 avocado, cut in half and stoned/pitted

## Miso-ginger Dipping Sauce

170 g/½ cup white miso paste

1 teaspoon grated fresh ginger

1 tablespoon grated orange zest

## Variation Fillings

1 yellow (bell) pepper

1 small carrot, finely sliced

12–15 young asparagus spears

1–2 pickled beetroots/beets, finely sliced

## Serves 4

Firstly, mix all of the ingredients for the miso-ginger dipping sauce together with 4 tablespoons of water in a small bowl. Cover and set aside.

Next, make your 'sushi rice' by combining the cauliflower rice with the rice vinegar, nama shoyu and lemon juice in a large mixing bowl.

Lay out one sheet of nori, place 2 heaped tablespoons of the sushi rice along the bottom side of the sheet, about 2½ cm/1 inch up from the edge; layer a few strips of red (bell) pepper, spring onion/scallion and enoki mushrooms onto the rice, then roll your seaweed around the filling. You may want to seal your roll by dabbing a little water along the edge.

Slice the avocado flesh into long, fine strips whilst still in the skin, and then make a cut widthways through the avocado. Carefully remove the avocado slices from the skin and fan out along the top of your sushi roll, covering it completely.

Repeat the process until you have used all of the ingredients – you should have enough to make about 4 more rolls. Finally, cut your rolls into 6 pieces each and serve with the miso-ginger dipping sauce.

## Variations

Make these rolls in the same way, replacing the red (bell) pepper, spring onions/scallions and enoki mushrooms with young asparagus spears, yellow (bell) pepper and carrot for an alternative flavour combination (pictured: opposite, top right). Or try hand-rolling the sushi rice into bite-sized pieces, top with a very thin slice of pickled beetroot/beet and wrap with a band of nori (pictured: opposite, bottom).

---

**NUTRITIONAL INFORMATION**

**Per serving:** 256 kcals/1068 kJ, 10.9 g fat (1.8 g saturated), 15.8 g protein, 16.3 g carbs (4.9 g sugars), 4.7 g salt, 15.2 g fibre

---

# Lettuce Rolls with Sticky Mustard Dipping Sauce

Sometimes you need to be able to eat lunch with one hand. But that doesn't mean it has to be all carrot sticks and houmous all the time (though I do love them!). These lettuce rolls are a good way to switch up lunch in a pinch.

2 heads Little Gem/Bibb (or other soft) lettuce

2 carrots

3 tomatoes, deseeded and thinly sliced

1 yellow (bell) pepper, thinly sliced

30 g/¾ cup pea shoots

75 g/½ cup sunflower seeds, soaked for at least 4 hours

3 tablespoons chopped fresh flat-leaf parsley

2 sticks celery, chopped

3 spring onions/scallions, chopped

2 tablespoons soy sauce (or nama shoyu or Bragg liquid aminos)

freshly squeezed juice of 1 lemon

## Sticky Mustard Dipping Sauce

60 ml/¼ cup olive oil

60 ml/¼ cup honey (or use agave or maple syrup)

1 tablespoon smooth French mustard

freshly ground black pepper, to taste

## Serves 4

Using a fork, mix all the sticky mustard dipping sauce ingredients together in a small mixing bowl and set aside.

Remove the outer leaves of the lettuce and set aside (you will need about 12 leaves). Shred the rest of the lettuce along with the carrots, and combine with the tomatoes, yellow (bell) pepper and pea shoots in a large mixing bowl.

Rinse the sunflower seeds and put them in a food processor with the parsley, celery and spring onions/scallions. Add the soy sauce and the lemon juice and pulse until smooth.

To build the rolls, layer about 2 tablespoons of the sunflower seed mixture in the bottom of each leaf and top with a generous amount of the shredded vegetables. Serve alongside the dipping sauce – you should be able to easily pick up and roll the edges of the leaves around the filling to dip in the sauce.

---

### NUTRITIONAL INFORMATION

**Per serving:** (if using honey) 366 kcals/kJ 1527, 21.2 g fat (3 g saturated), 8.3 g protein, 32.8 g carbs (27.1 g sugars), 1.3 g salt, 5.8 g fibre

---

# NOT-YOUR-AVERAGE WRAP

2 large chard leaves
1 large papaya (or 2 small
    papayas), peeled and sliced
1 mango, peeled, stoned/pitted
    and sliced
2 avocados, peeled, stoned/
    pitted and sliced
a large handful of alfalfa sprouts
a small handful of beansprouts
6 tablespoons crushed almonds,
    (or other nut of choice), plus
    1 tablespoon, for topping

## MISO–SESAME DRESSING
2 teaspoons brown miso paste
2 tablespoons toasted sesame oil

## SERVES 2

To me, chard is nature's way of giving us the convenience of a sandwich, all contained and no clean-up necessary, without the need for refined carbohydrates. You can pretty much use chard as a wrap for any of your favourite sandwich fillings. This papaya and avocado wrap is particularly fun, but experiment with whatever it is you crave.

Using a sharp knife, lay your chard leaves out flat and cut in half down the middle, discarding the stems completely.

Place a quarter of the papaya, mango, avocado, alfalfa sprouts and beansprouts down the middle of each halved chard leaf. Sprinkle the nuts over the mixture and roll the chard leaf around the mixture as you would for a sandwich wrap.

For the dressing, whisk the miso paste and sesame oil together in a small mixing bowl. Pour over the top of the chard wraps, sprinkle with extra crushed nuts and serve immediately.

NUTRITIONAL INFORMATION
**Per serving:** 396 kcals/1639 kJ, 31.3 g fat (4.7 g saturated), 8.9 g protein, 15.8 g carbs (13.1 g sugars), 0.4 g salt, 7.6 g fibre

# Macadamia Cheese

Cheese is often the hardest thing for people to part with when contemplating going dairy-free. It certainly was for me, until I discovered that you could make quite authentic substitutes using nuts and seeds. Use this recipe as a blueprint and play around with the flavourings, amount of water, and shape to create unlimited variations. If you use cashews, add a little less water and let the probiotics sit for less time to create more of a hard cheese. You can use pretty much any nuts or seeds you like, too, as long as you soak them beforehand.

140 g/2 cups macadamia nuts
about 250 ml/1 cup warm water
2 probiotic supplement capsules (such as Acidophilus or a broad-spectrum probiotic)
½ teaspoon sea salt
1 tablespoon nutritional yeast
2 tablespoons black olives, chopped
1 tablespoon lemon juice
seed crackers, to serve

*a high-speed blender*

*a colander lined with cheesecloth/muslin*

Serves 2

Put the macadamia nuts in a high-speed blender with just enough warm water to cover them. Tip in the contents of the probiotic capsules and blend slowly until you have a completely smooth but thick mixture – if it easily forms peaks when a fork is dipped into the mixture, you know you're on the right track, but ensure the blender is switched off at the mains before testing.

Pour the mixture into the lined colander, fold the edges of the cloth over the top and press down gently to squeeze any excess moisture out of the nut mixture. Place a small plate on top of it and something heavy (a filled jar, can or book) on top of that. Leave the mixture to sit at room temperature for at least 24 hours to give it time to ferment and develop that 'cheesy' flavour.

Transfer the fermented nut mixture to a bowl and stir in the sea salt, nutritional yeast, chopped black olives and lemon juice.

Lay a sheet of clingfilm/plastic wrap on a clean work surface and tip the nut mixture out onto it. Wrap the clingfilm/plastic wrap around the mixture and roll to shape into a log. Twist the ends to seal and chill in the fridge for about 6 hours before serving with seed crackers.

---

**NUTRITIONAL INFORMATION**
**Per serving:** 568 kcals/2341 kJ, 54.6 g fat (8.8 g saturated), 9.4 g protein, 5.8 g carbs (3.4 g sugars), 2 g salt, 7.9 g fibre

---

# Bibimbap Cabbage Wraps

The novelty of superfoods sometimes takes us away from appreciating the local produce that lies right under our noses. Take cabbage; it's a cruciferous vegetable that is crammed with vitamins C and K. These simple veggies found in our back gardens are the real food as medicine.

100 g/½ cup wild rice

350 g/7 cups spinach

45 g/¾ cup beansprouts

3 tablespoons soy sauce

80 ml/⅓ cup sesame oil

30 g/1 cup shiitake mushrooms

1 white onion, sliced

2 garlic cloves, crushed
   separately

olive oil, for frying

1 Chinese leaf cabbage

½ tablespoon granulated stevia

2 teaspoons chilli/chili (hot
   pepper) paste

2 tablespoons rice wine vinegar
   (or apple cider vinegar)

1 heaped tablespoon gochujang
   (available in Korean
   supermarkets or online),
   to serve

2 radishes, finely sliced, to serve

### Serves 4

Bring about 750 ml/3 cups of water to the boil over a medium–high heat. Add a pinch of salt and return to the boil. Put the wild rice in the water, reduce the heat and simmer for about 45 minutes.

Meanwhile, bring another saucepan or pot of water to the boil and place a metal colander over the top. Put the spinach in the colander, cover and steam until cooked through. Immediately submerse the spinach in a bowl of ice-cold water. Drain and set aside.

Steam the beansprouts in the same way. Drain then mix with 1 tablespoon of the soy sauce and set aside.

Pour about 3 tablespoons of the sesame oil into a wok and set over a medium–high heat. Add 1 tablespoon of soy sauce along with the shiitake mushrooms and stir-fry. Transfer to a bowl and set aside.

Next, using the same wok, stir-fry the onion with 1 crushed garlic clove, a drizzle of olive oil and 1 tablespoon of the soy sauce. Transfer to the bowl with the mushrooms and set aside.

Slice the Chinese leaf cabbage into strips, saving 6–8 of the larger leaves for serving. Toss the strips into the same wok, this time adding the stevia, chilli/chili paste, rice wine vinegar, the other crushed garlic clove and 1 tablespoon of the sesame oil. Cook until the cabbage softens.

Assemble the wraps by lining the bottom of each reserved cabbage leaf with wild rice. Drizzle the drained spinach with the remaining sesame oil and top each leaf. Add a little of each of the vegetable components and serve with the gochujang and a few slices of radish scattered over.

---

### NUTRITIONAL INFORMATION
**Per serving:** 289 kcals/1204 kJ, 16.5 g fat (2.3 g saturated), 9.2 g protein, 22.1 g carbs (7 g sugars), 2.3 g salt, 7.6 g fibre

# Hemp Tabbouleh with Pea and Mint Falafel

## Hemp Tabbouleh

80 g/2 cups fresh flat-leaf
   parsley, finely chopped
10 g/¼ cup fresh mint, finely
   chopped
a handful of finely chopped kale
1 large tomato, finely diced
½ white onion, finely diced
a 10-cm/4-inch piece of
   cucumber, finely diced
freshly squeezed juice of 1 lemon
2½ tablespoons olive oil, plus
   extra for the falafel
4 tablespoons hemp seeds
2 heaped tablespoons
   pomegranate seeds
sea salt

## Pea and Mint Falafel

150 g/1 cup cooked peas
10 g/¼ cup fresh mint, chopped
1 garlic clove
4 tablespoons chopped spring
   onion/scallion
¼ teaspoon bicarbonate of/
   baking soda
2 teaspoons freshly squeezed
   lemon juice

## Lemon Tahini Sauce

115 g/⅓ cup light tahini
1 tablespoon freshly squeezed
   lemon juice

*a baking sheet, lined with foil
   and greased*

## Serves 2

Using peas, which contain an amazing 13% protein, instead of chickpeas to make these falafel mean they are a lot easier to digest. If you want to start your kids on eating green things, or if you just want to add some more into your own diet, these falafel are a great transition food, full of guilty delicious taste and good-for-you greens! The key to an authentic tabbouleh is to chop your ingredients (particularly the parsley) as finely as possible.

Toss the chopped parsley, mint and kale together in a large mixing bowl, then add the tomato, onion and cucumber. Pour in the lemon juice and olive oil and mix well. Add the hemp and pomegranate seeds and season with salt. Set aside.

Preheat the oven to 200°C (400°F) Gas 6.

Combine all of the falafel ingredients in a food processor and pulse until well incorporated, but still have a little texture.

Divide the mixture into 6–8 pieces and roll each one into a ball. Place on the prepared baking sheet, then press down gently in the centre of each ball to form an indent.

Lightly brush the tops of the falafel with olive oil. Bake in the preheated oven for 15 minutes, flip the falafel over and bake for another 10 minutes.

Meanwhile, to make the sauce, mix the tahini and lemon juice together with 1 tablespoon of water, using a whisk.

Serve the warm pea and mint falafel on a bed of hemp tabbouleh and drizzled with the lemon tahini sauce.

### NUTRITIONAL INFORMATION
Per serving: 794 kcals/3289 kJ, 61.2 g fat (8.3 g saturated), 28.5 g protein, 22.9 g carbs (11.3 g sugars), 1 g salt, 19.2 g fibre

# EVENING FEASTS

Dinnertime is a time to kick back and enjoy yourself;
I'm a big believer in taking that time to relax over
a nice meal as the day comes to a close. Just because
you want a healthy dinner, it doesn't mean you can't
have that daily moment of celebration and appreciation.
These dishes feel like proper meals, meals you can take
an hour to eat in front of a movie, or share over long
conversations with loved ones.

# FUSION NOODLES

This dish started by total accident – it was one of those use-whatever's-in-the-fridge meals that came together when I was craving every flavour – spicy, tangy, creamy, salty. I called them 'fusion' because they incorporate tastes from all over the world – tahini from the Middle East, Asian soy sauce, a Creole-style mix of dried spices, as well as hot sauce, which is common in many areas of the world. The lime ties the whole thing together and somehow, it works.

680 g/24 oz. kelp noodles, soaked overnight
10 asparagus spears, cut into 3-cm/1¼-inch pieces
2 carrots
2 tablespoons Bragg liquid aminos (or tamari soy sauce)
1 tablespoon sesame oil (or olive oil)
225 g/¾ cup tahini
2 tablespoons sriracha (or other hot sauce)
1 bay leaf
½ teaspoon ground cumin
½ teaspoon dried oregano
½ teaspoon paprika
a pinch of salt (optional)
2 limes
370 g/4 generous cups beansprouts
1 red chilli/chile, finely chopped
a spiralizer (optional)

SERVES 2–4

Using kitchen scissors, cut the kelp noodles down to the size of regular noodles – they tend to come very long which makes them hard to work with.

Bring a saucepan or pot of water to the boil over a medium–high heat. Add the asparagus pieces and cook until softened.

Next, prepare the carrots by slicing them using a spiralizer. Alternatively, slice them very thinly lengthways with a sharp knife.

Put the carrot strips in a frying pan/skillet and set over a medium heat. Add the liquid aminos and sesame oil, and stir. Add the soaked kelp noodles, then mix in your tahini, sriracha and dried herbs and spices. I find this recipe plenty salty already, but add a little to taste if you wish. Squeeze in the juice of one of the limes, and finally, add the cooked asparagus and beansprouts.

Toss everything together so that the noodles are well coated in sauce. Remove the bay leaf and divide the noodles between 2–4 bowls, depending on whether you are serving them alone or as an accompaniment to another dish. Top each bowl with a small handful of chopped red chilli/chile and enjoy with an extra squeeze of lime, to taste.

> NUTRITIONAL INFORMATION
> Per serving: 937 kcals/3875 kJ, 74.1 g fat (10.7 g saturated), 36.1 g protein, 19.4 g carbs (14.5 g sugars), 3.3 g salt, 24.2 g fibre

# Spicy Sweet Potato Moussaka

One-dish meals are so handy if you're cooking for your family or if you're a fan of prepping your meals for the week ahead. One serving of this moussaka will provide two servings of vegetables in a pretty painless way and doubles up perfectly as lunchbox meals until you've worked through the whole bake.

1 medium aubergine/eggplant

2 courgettes/zucchini

400 g/3½ cups peeled and diced sweet potato

2 garlic cloves, crushed

½ teaspoon cayenne pepper

½ teaspoon ground chipotle powder

freshly squeezed juice of 1 lime

180 g/1½ cups macadamia nuts, soaked for at least 2 hours

85 g/¾ cup sun-dried tomatoes in oil, drained

1 teaspoon ground cumin

1 tablespoon freshly squeezed lemon juice (or apple cider vinegar)

1 teaspoon salt

2 baking sheets, greased

a high-speed blender

a 25 x 30-cm/10 x 12-inch casserole dish

SERVES 8

Preheat the oven to 180°C (350°F) Gas 4.

Slice the aubergine/eggplant and courgette/zucchini into rounds about 1 cm/³⁄₈ inch thick. Arrange on the prepared baking sheets and bake in the preheated oven for 15 minutes. Remove from the oven and set aside to cool, but keep the oven on.

Meanwhile, boil the sweet potato cubes in a large pot of water set over a medium–high heat for about 16 minutes, until soft. Drain and mash the sweet potato and mix in the crushed garlic, cayenne, chipotle powder and lime juice.

Put the macadamia nuts, sun-dried tomatoes, cumin, lemon juice and salt in a blender and pulse until smooth.

Once you have prepared all of the components, it's time to assemble the casserole. Place about 3 tablespoons of the sweet potato mixture at the bottom of the casserole dish and spread thinly – it doesn't matter if it doesn't cover the entire surface. Layer some of the baked aubergine/eggplant first, then spread a generous layer of the sweet potato mixture on top. Cover this with a layer of courgette/zucchini, then some of the macadamia spread. Repeat until you have used up all of the ingredients, finishing with a thick layer of the macadamia mixture.

Cover the moussaka with foil and bake in the still-warm oven for 20 minutes, then remove the foil and bake for another 15 minutes.

### NUTRITIONAL INFORMATION
Per serving: 259 kcals/1073 kJ, 19.1 g fat (3.1 g saturated), 4.1 g protein, 14.8 g carbs (5 g sugars), 0.8 g salt, 5.5 g fibre

# Summery Noodles with Spiced Almond Butter

Cucumber is one of the most underrated vegetables in my opinion – it's more alkalizing than leafy greens and one of the only ways to get a decent dose of silica, which encourages plump, young-looking skin.

60 ml/¼ cup red wine vinegar

4 tablespoons olive oil

30 g/1 cup enoki (or shimeji, or shiitake) mushrooms

1 large cucumber

2 carrots, finely sliced

6 spring onions/scallions, finely sliced

¼ red cabbage, finely sliced

2 yellow (bell) peppers, finely sliced

1 red chilli/chile, finely sliced

## Spiced Almond Butter

1 red chilli/chile, deseeded and diced

85 g/heaped ¼ cup almond butter

125 ml/½ cup coconut aminos (or apple cider vinegar)

2 tablespoons Bragg liquid aminos (or tamari or soy sauce)

1 teaspoon tamarind paste

freshly squeezed juice of 1 lemon

*a spiralizer (optional)*

*a high-speed blender*

## Serves 2

In a shallow dish, mix the red wine vinegar and olive oil. Put the mushrooms in the mixture to soften.

Next, prepare the cucumber by slicing it using a spiralizer. Alternatively, slice it very thinly lengthways with a sharp knife. Divide the cucumber noodles between serving bowls and top with sliced carrots, spring onions/scallions, cabbage and (bell) peppers.

Put the chilli/chile in a blender with the rest of the spiced almond butter ingredients and blend until smooth.

Top each bowl of noodles with the marinated mushrooms; you can also pour on some of the extra marinade depending on how saucy you like your noodles. Finish with sliced red chilli/chile and serve with the spiced almond butter on the side.

> **NUTRITIONAL INFORMATION**
> Per serving: 889 kcals/3679 kJ, 71.2 g fat (9.9 g saturated), 21.5 g protein, 30.3 g carbs (24.6 g sugars), 2 g salt, 20.7 g fibre

# Neatballs

90 g/1½ cups brown mushrooms

75 g/½ cup sunflower seeds, soaked for at least 1 hour

70 g/⅔ cup sun-dried tomatoes, soaked for at least 2 hours

⅓ red onion

1 teaspoon ground cumin

½ teaspoon dried oregano

½ teaspoon ground coriander

1 tablespoon freshly squeezed lemon juice

2 garlic cloves

1 tablespoon white miso

a splash of soy sauce

## Tomato Sauce

2 tablespoons olive oil

1 onion, sliced

1 garlic clove, crushed

1 teaspoon *ras el hanout*

1 tablespoon tomato purée/paste

400 g/2 cups canned chopped tomatoes

1 carrot, grated

75 g/½ cup dried apricots, chopped

300 ml/1¼ cups vegetable stock

## To Serve

150 g/1 cup cooked quinoa

80 g/1 cup flaked/slivered almonds

a small bunch of fresh mint, chopped

### Serves 2–4

When I first became vegan, I got overly excited about the idea that I could make plant-based 'meatballs'. The problem was that they were either made using mostly soy and processed faux-meat products, or the raw vegan versions were made entirely of seeds and nuts – both of which are gut bombs. These 'neatballs' are lightened-up but still hearty, because I use brown mushrooms as the main component.

Preheat the oven to 180°C (350°F) Gas 4.

Put the mushrooms in a food processor and pulse until you have a mixture that resembles the texture of ground meat. Transfer to a large mixing bowl and set aside.

Separately, pulse all of the other ingredients together until you have a smooth but still chunky mixture. Add to the ground mushroom mixture and mix together by hand.

Roll the mixture into meatball-sized balls, place on a baking sheet and bake in the preheated oven for about 1 hour, until the outsides are crispy.

Meanwhile, to make the tomato sauce, heat the olive oil in a frying pan/skillet set over a medium heat. Add the sliced onion, crushed garlic and *ras el hanout*, and fry for 3–5 minutes. Add the tomato purée/paste and cook for another minute. Add the remaining ingredients, reduce the heat, cover and simmer for 10 minutes, until thickened.

Serve the neatballs with the tomato sauce on a bed of quinoa, sprinkled with flaked/slivered almonds and chopped mint.

---

**NUTRITIONAL INFORMATION**
Per serving: 633 kcals/2766 kJ, 33.1 g fat (4.9 g saturated), 23.9 g protein, 58.5 g carbs (44.1 g sugars), 1.4 g salt, 17.8 g fibre

# GRILLED ROMAINE HEARTS WITH RANCH DRESSING

Who knew that you could grill lettuce? I certainly didn't. But you can and you can grill other salad greens like avocado too! Try it with a squeeze of lemon and a pinch of salt. If you want to elevate standard salad flavours, the grilling technique adds a nice smoky taste and I love it when paired with this creamy ranch dressing. Grilled romaine would also work well in a warm salmon Niçoise salad.

1 large head romaine lettuce, quartered lengthways

1½ tablespoons olive oil

50 g/½ cup green beans

120 g/½ cup artichokes in olive oil, drained and roughly chopped

85 g/½ cup almonds, chopped, to serve

## RANCH DRESSING

170 g/1 cup skinless almonds

1 tablespoon lemon olive oil (or olive oil)

2 tablespoons freshly squeezed lemon juice

1 tablespoon chopped fresh flat-leaf parsley

1 tablespoon chopped fresh chives

a pinch of salt

a pinch of garlic powder

½ teaspoon onion powder

*a high-speed blender*

## SERVES 2

Begin by preparing the ranch dressing. Put the almonds in a small bowl and cover with water. Leave to soak for at least 2 hours, or ideally overnight. Drain the almonds and rinse well. Put the soaked almonds in a blender with 80 ml/⅓ cup of water and blend until completely smooth. Add the remaining ingredients and blend again until they're fully incorporated in the dressing. With the motor running, drizzle in a little extra water if necessary to thin out.

Preheat the grill/broiler to medium.

Brush the romaine quarters with the olive oil and grill/broil for 5–7 minutes, until lightly browned.

Meanwhile, steam the green beans in a metal colander set over a saucepan or pot of boiling water for 3–4 minutes, until tender.

Transfer the romaine quarters to serving dishes (two quarters would be a generous serving for one person) and scatter the steamed green beans and artichokes over the top. Scatter over the chopped almonds, drizzle with ranch dressing and serve immediately.

> **NUTRITIONAL INFORMATION**
> Per serving: 752 kcals/3111 kJ,
> 63.5 g fat (6.2 g saturated),
> 27.2 g protein, 14.2 g carbs (10.3 g
> sugars), 0.7 g salt, 7.7 g fibre

# Oodles of Zoodles

'Zoodles' or courgette/zucchini noodles, are gaining in popularity as an alternative to traditional pastas. They look exactly like spaghetti and can be used in the same way to provide an everyday spaghetti-lite. These are delicious served with a simple red or green pesto.

2 medium courgettes/zucchini, trimmed
sea salt and freshly ground black pepper, to season
a handful of fresh basil, to serve

### Red Pesto
60 g/tightly packed $^1\!/_2$ cup sun-dried tomatoes in oil, drained
125 g/1 cup pine nuts
1 roasted garlic clove
3–4 tablespoons olive oil
$^1\!/_2$ teaspoon dried basil
$^1\!/_4$ teaspoon dried oregano

### Macadamia 'Parmesan'
60 g/$^1\!/_2$ cup macadamia nuts
4 tablespoons nutritional yeast
$^1\!/_4$ teaspoon salt
a spiralizer

Serves 4

Begin by preparing the zoodles. Slice the courgettes/zucchini using a spiralizer and set aside until you are ready to serve.

To make the red pesto, put all of the ingredients in a food processor with a little black pepper and pulse until smooth, adding more olive oil to loosen the mixture if necessary. Transfer to a bowl and set aside.

Rinse the food processor and pulse all of the macadamia 'Parmesan' ingredients together to a fine crumb.

When you are ready to serve, bring a saucepan or pot of water to the boil over a medium–high heat. Add the zoodles and cook for 2 minutes, taking care not to let them overcook. Drain in a fine mesh sieve/strainer and return the zoodles to the pan. Add 1 tablespoon of the red pesto to the pan and set over a gentle heat for 1 minute to warm the pesto.

Warm the remaining red pesto in a separate saucepan or pot set over a gentle heat for 2–3 minutes.

Divide the mixture between two bowls, top with the warm red pesto and sprinkle over the macadamia 'Parmesan'. Garnish each with a few fresh basil leaves and serve.

NUTRITIONAL INFORMATION
Per serving: 768 kcals/3165 kJ, 74.6 g fat (10.9 g saturated), 13.8 g protein, 6.9 g carbs (2.6 g sugars), 0.7 g salt, 6.8g fibre

# Portobello Pizza Caps

In macrobiotic cuisine, mushrooms aren't classified as vegetables: they have their own category due to the fact that they boast such different properties. Not only do they have medicinal uses that boost our immunity, but they are also one of the only food sources of vitamin D, which we are collectively deficient in. Everyone would benefit from consuming more of these humble veggie superstars, and these pizza caps are a fun way to introduce more of them.

80 g/²/₃ cup cashew or pine nuts, plus extra for toasting

6 tablespoons nutritional yeast

12 fresh basil leaves, plus extra to garnish

3 tablespoons olive oil

1 tablespoon freshly squeezed lemon juice

¹/₄ teaspoon salt

4 portobello mushrooms, washed and stems removed

4 tablespoons tomato purée/paste

8 black olives, stoned/pitted and finely sliced

¹/₂ green (bell) pepper, finely sliced

¹/₄ red onion, finely sliced

80 g/2 cups mixed green salad leaves, to serve

a baking sheet, greased and lined with foil

SERVES 4 AS AN APPETIZER, OR 2 AS A MAIN

Begin by preparing the filling. Put the cashew or pine nuts in a small bowl and cover with water. Leave to soak for at least 2 hours, or ideally overnight. Drain the nuts and rinse well. Put the soaked nuts in a food processor with the nutritional yeast, basil, 2 tablespoons of the olive oil, lemon juice and salt, and pulse until smooth.

Preheat the oven to 190°C (375°F) Gas 5.

Lightly brush the tops of the mushrooms with the remaining olive oil and place them top down on the prepared baking sheet. You can make hollow rings to sit the mushrooms into by twisting a strip of foil – use them as holders for the caps, so they don't touch the baking sheet and overcook.

Spread each cap with 1 tablespoon of tomato purée/paste, then top with the nut mixture and the sliced olives, pepper and onion.

Bake in the preheated oven for 20–25 minutes.

Meanwhile, lightly toast some extra pine nuts in a dry frying pan/skillet set over a medium heat.

Remove the portobello pizza caps from the oven and serve warm with a mixed green salad, sprinkled with the toasted pine nuts.

---

**NUTRITIONAL INFORMATION**
**Per serving:** 308 kcals/1279 kJ, 20.1 g fat (3.8 g saturated), 17.9 g protein, 9.9 g carbs (4.3 g sugars), 1.3 g salt, 7.7 g fibre

# Chilli Rellenos

Chilli Rellenos are one of Mexico's most emblematic dishes. Traditionally made using a mix of Spanish and local ingredients, they are often stuffed with meats and cheeses, then fried. This is definitely a liberal take on the original, but still retains all the flavour and heat that the dish is known for.

½ red onion, finely diced

1 tablespoon olive oil, plus extra for brushing

1 medium tomato, chopped

65 g/1 cup brown mushrooms, chopped

150 g/¾ cup ready-made tomato pasta sauce

1 tablespoon tomato purée/paste

1 tablespoon balsamic vinegar

1 teaspoon vegan Worcestershire sauce (such as Biona Organic)

½ teaspoon chilli powder (or the flesh of 1 fresh chilli/chile)

a generous dash of hot (pepper) sauce, to taste

30 g/⅓ cup walnuts, plus extra chopped, to serve

3 pointed red peppers, halved and deseeded

freshly ground black pepper

chopped fresh coriander/cilantro, to garnish

a baking sheet, greased and lined with foil

Serves 2–3

Preheat the oven to 200°C (400°F) Gas 6.

Put the red onion and olive oil in a frying pan/skillet set over medium heat. Fry until browned, then add the chopped tomato and mushrooms, tomato pasta sauce, tomato purée/paste, balsamic vinegar, Worcestershire sauce, chilli powder and hot (pepper) sauce. Season with black pepper, then simmer for a few minutes, allowing the mixture to reduce slightly.

Remove from the heat and transfer to a food processor with the walnuts and pulse lightly – you want the mixture to be a little chunky.

Lightly brush the outsides of the pepper halves with olive oil and place them skin-side down on the prepared baking sheet. Spoon the tomato mixture into the pepper halves and bake in the preheated oven for 35 minutes, until brown.

Remove the peppers from the oven and garnish with coriander/cilantro and chopped walnuts before serving.

### NUTRITIONAL INFORMATION
Per serving: 314 kcals/1308 kJ, 17.5 g fat (2.3 g saturated), 8.6 g protein, 26.2 g carbs (24.1 g sugars), 0.5 g salt, 9.1 g fibre

# WILD RICE SALAD

I'm including this dish because I make it often for get-togethers and people go crazy for it! Wild rice is actually a grass rather than a grain – so it is technically Paleo-friendly. If you'd rather not include wild rice in your plan, feel free to substitute it here with quinoa, cauliflower rice (see page 73), or a generous mound of shredded carrot, which tastes delicious alongside the flavours of this dish!

100 g/1 cup wild rice

1 pomegranate

2 avocados, peeled, stoned/
   pitted and diced

300 g/2 cups cherry tomatoes,
   halved

a bunch of fresh flat-leaf parsley,
   roughly chopped

## STICKY MUSTARD DRESSING

¾ tablespoons grain mustard

5 tablespoons olive oil

2 teaspoons honey (or use agave
   or maple syrup)

½ teaspoon salt

freshly squeezed juice of 1 lemon

## SERVES 4

Bring a saucepan or pot of water to the boil over a medium–high heat. Add the wild rice, reduce the heat and simmer for about 40 minutes, until completely soft.

To extract the seeds from the pomegranate, cut it into large sections and put in a large bowl filled with water. The seeds should float to the top, leaving the flesh to sink to the bottom.

Combine the pomegranate seeds with the avocado, cherry tomatoes and parsley in a large mixing bowl.

To make the sticky mustard dressing, mix all of the ingredients together in a bowl and whisk with a fork.

Once the wild rice is fully cooked, drain in a fine mesh sieve/strainer and rinse under cold running water to cool. Add to the salad mixture with the sticky mustard dressing and stir until all the ingredients are well coated.

Serve immediately.

---

**NUTRITIONAL INFORMATION**

**Per serving:** (if using honey) 412 kcals/1707 kJ, 29.1 g fat (5.1 g saturated), 6 g protein, 26.8 g carbs (14.2 g sugars), 0.9 g salt, 9.4 g fibre

---

# Raw Curry with Jicama Rice

We tend to think of curry as a cheat meal but, when you think about it, there are a lot of healthy things in it: good fats from the coconut milk, warming and stimulating spices, all mixed in with tonnes of fresh veggies and herbs. This version features all of these good parts without the unnecessary sugars that sneak into curry sauces. I also substitute the white rice for jicama rice; if you can't find jicama, try cauliflower rice (see page 73) instead.

1 large jicama/water chestnut, roughly chopped

1 tablespoon mirin (optional)

1 small courgette/zucchini, finely sliced

12 okra, finely sliced

1 large carrot, finely sliced

2 large handfuls beansprouts

1 young Thai coconut (or 400 g/ 2 cups full-fat coconut milk, but this isn't raw)

1 red (bell) pepper, deseeded

1 tomato

1 garlic clove

1 small Thai chilli/jalapeño

1 lemongrass stalk

1 heaped teaspoon curry powder

2 spring onions/scallions

freshly squeezed juice of 1 lime

a 2½-cm/1-inch piece of fresh ginger, plus extra grated to garnish

a large handful of fresh coriander/cilantro, plus extra to garnish

*a high-speed blender*

SERVES 2

Begin by blending the jicama in a food processor to a fine rice-like texture. 1 large jicama should yield about 900 g/3 cups jicama rice.

Mix the jicama rice with the mirin (if using), cover and set aside.

Put the sliced courgette/zucchini, okra and carrot in a large mixing bowl with the beansprouts and set aside.

Carefully cut the coconut open, scoop out the meat and the water, and put both in a blender with the rest of the ingredients. Blend until smooth, then pour the mixture over the mixed vegetables. Mix well, cover and set aside for 2 hours at room temperature to allow the flavours to infuse and soften the vegetables before consuming.

To serve, divide the rice between two serving bowls and top with the curry mixture. Garnish with grated ginger and a sprig of coriander/cilantro and enjoy.

---

### NUTRITIONAL INFORMATION
**Per serving:** 527 kcals/2192 kJ, 21.5 g fat (17.3 g saturated), 11.9 g protein, 50.6 g carbs (32.4 g sugars), 0.5 g salt, 41.8 g fibre

---

100 g/1 cup quinoa flour

450 g/4 cups sweet potatoes, peeled and boiled

60 ml/¼ cup almond milk

2 tablespoons olive oil

½ teaspoon salt, plus extra for boiling

½ teaspoon garlic powder

1 teaspoon xanthan gum

balsamic vinegar, to serve

### Red Pepper Sauce

2 red (bell) peppers

4 large tomatoes (I use roma tomatoes)

4 tablespoons olive oil

2 garlic cloves

½ white onion, sliced

80 g/1 cup fresh basil

sea salt and freshly ground black pepper, to taste

*a handheld electric mixer*

*a high-speed blender*

### Serves 4

# Sweet Potato Gnocchi

Substituting sweet potato and a small amount of healthy flour is a straightforward way to make delicious gnocchi.

Preheat the oven to 110°C (225°F) Gas ¼. Spread the quinoa flour evenly over a baking sheet and toast in the preheated oven for 2½ hours.

To make the gnocchi, put the boiled sweet potatoes in a large mixing bowl. Pour in the almond milk and olive oil, then whisk using an electric mixer, until fluffy. Tip the mixture out onto a clean worksurface. In a separate bowl, mix together the toasted quinoa flour, salt, garlic powder and xanthan gum. Add half of the flour mixture to the sweet potato and knead to combine; repeat with the second half. Split the dough into 3 equal pieces and roll out each piece into a long thin strip, about 2½–4 cm/1–1½ inches thick. Chop thumb-sized pieces of dough and press them lightly with a fork. Using your index finger, roll one long side of the gnocchi over the other, so that it curls.

For the red pepper sauce, preheat the oven to 200°C (400°F) Gas 6. Brush the peppers and 3 of the tomatoes with a little olive oil and roast them with the garlic cloves in the preheated oven for 35–40 minutes. Meanwhile, fry the onion in a little oil in a saucepan or pot set over a medium heat, until brown. Remove the vegetables from the oven and peel the skins off the peppers and tomatoes. Transfer to a blender and pulse until smooth. Add the remaining raw tomato, fried onion, half of the basil, remaining olive oil, and pulse again. Transfer the mixture to a pan, season with salt and pepper and warm through.

Cook the gnocchi in a pot of boiling water for about 2 minutes – the gnocchi will bob to the top of the pan when cooked. Remove from the pan using a slotted spoon and drain on paper towels. Serve hot with the red pepper sauce and garnish with the leftover basil and a drizzle of balsamic vinegar.

### NUTRITIONAL INFORMATION

Per serving: 391 kcals/1634, 18.9 g fat (2.8 g saturated), 6.8 g protein, 44.6 g carbs (19 g sugars), 1.6 g salt, 7.9 g fibre

# AUBERGINE STEAKS WITH CAULI-MASH

If you asked me to give you five easy eats to keep firmly in your healthy eating arsenal, cauli-mash would be at the top! If every time you were craving potatoes you could whip up some of this instead, that would add up to a huge change. Pair it with these hearty aubergine/eggplant steaks and some sautéed vegetables for a real 'meat and two veg' treat.

1 large aubergine/eggplant
60 ml/¼ cup low-sodium soy sauce (or nama shoyu or Bragg liquid aminos)
60 ml/¼ cup mirin
2 tablespoons balsamic vinegar
3 spring onions/scallions, sliced, plus extra to serve
olive oil spray (or other cooking spray)

## CAULI-MASH

1 head cauliflower, roughly chopped
3 garlic cloves
3 tablespoons olive oil, plus extra to serve
2 teaspoons chopped fresh chives
½ teaspoon chopped fresh thyme
salt and freshly ground black pepper

## SERVES 2-3

Slice the aubergine/eggplant into rounds, about a 13 mm/½ inch thick and place them in a casserole dish.

Mix the soy sauce, mirin, balsamic vinegar and spring onions/scallions together in a small bowl, then heat in a frying pan/skillet set over a medium heat for a few minutes, allowing the liquid to thicken slightly.

Pour the soy marinade over the aubergine/eggplant rounds in the casserole dish. Make sure the aubergine/eggplant is fully covered and set aside to let the vegetables soak up the flavour for at least 2 hours, ideally 4.

To make the cauli-mash, preheat the oven to 200°C (400°F) Gas 6. Steam the cauliflower in a metal colander set over a pan of boiling water, until soft. Roast the 3 garlic cloves with the skin on in the preheated oven. Remove the skin and put the garlic in a food processor with the steamed cauliflower and the remaining ingredients. Pulse until the mixture is smooth and creamy, then chill in the fridge for 2 hours.

Set a clean, dry frying pan/skillet over a medium heat and spray it with olive oil. Sauté the marinated aubergine/eggplant slices in small batches, until they're all fully cooked.

Preheat the grill/broiler to medium, then grill/broil the sautéed aubergine/eggplant lightly for 5 minutes, for extra smokiness, if desired.

To serve, simply re-heat the cauli-mash in a preheated oven at 180°C (350°F) Gas 4 for 3–5 minutes. Spoon onto serving plates and top with the aubergine steaks. Sprinkle with spring onions/scallions and drizzle with olive oil.

---

**NUTRITIONAL INFORMATION**
Per serving: 406 kcals/1693 kJ, 20.7 g fat (3.2 g saturated), 13.1 g protein, 36.9 g carbs (22.6 g sugars), 3.5 g salt, 9.8 g fibre

# FEEL-GOOD TREATS

I guess now is a good time to share my favourite eating mantra with you: eat 90% for your body and 10% for your soul. If you want my advice, desserts should never be sworn off completely, even when you want a quick overhaul of your diet for an upcoming vacation, event or occasion. I always include a few treats in my daily diet plan. The reason? Because extremes are psychologically damaging and can permanently mess up our relationship with indulgence. As the mantra suggests, enjoying dessert from time to time is a health-enhancing practice. So grab a fork and get stuck in.

# Chocolate Orange Pie

Chocolate and orange is my favourite flavour combination when it comes to desserts. This pie looks elaborate but it's deceptively simple to make and delicious to eat.

## Base

500–650 g/3–4 cups almonds

60 g/$\frac{1}{2}$ cup dried figs (look for unsweetened/no added sugar)

3 tablespoons cacao nibs

1 tablespoon coconut oil

$\frac{1}{2}$ teaspoon pure vanilla extract

## Filling

155 g/1$\frac{1}{4}$ cups pine nuts, soaked overnight

$\frac{1}{2}$ tablespoon grated orange zest, plus a little extra to garnish

125 ml/$\frac{1}{2}$ cup freshly squeezed orange juice

90 g/$\frac{3}{4}$ cup raw cacao powder

60 ml/$\frac{1}{4}$ cup coconut oil

5 tablespoons granulated stevia (or up to 8 tablespoons for extra sweetness)

*a 23-cm/9-inch round springform cake pan, greased and lined with baking parchment*

## Serves 8–10

In a food processor, pulse all the base ingredients together until they form a thick paste. Scoop out the mixture and press it into the bottom of the cake pan. Put in the freezer to set.

Next, prepare the filling. Rinse your food processor and blend all of the ingredients together until completely smooth. Pour on top of your base and freeze again for at least 2 hours, to set.

Remove the pie from the freezer 20 minutes before serving. Sprinkle with extra orange zest to garnish and enjoy.

This pie will keep for up to 2 weeks in the freezer, and 3 days in the fridge, once defrosted.

---

**NUTRITIONAL INFORMATION**

Per serving: 691 kcals/2858 kJ, 60.6 g fat (12.9 g saturated), 22.8 g protein, 11.2 g carbs (8.4 g sugars), 0.3 g salt, 4.3 g fibre

# Nutty Nougat Cups

I used to love store-bought candy and confectionery – and you probably grew up with your favourites, too. Nowadays, I harness the nostalgia as inspiration to help me create new treats. This is a reimagining of a chocolate bar I used to adore, this time in cute cupcake form.

150 g/1 cups chopped
   dark/bittersweet chocolate
60 g/¹⁄₂ cup nuts of your choice,
   roughly chopped

## Nougat

110 g/1 cup almond meal
85 g/¹⁄₄ cup tahini
75 g/¹⁄₃ cup coconut sugar
2 tablespoons coconut oil
¹⁄₂ teaspoon pure vanilla extract

## Caramel

100 g/1 cup dates
1 tablespoon coconut oil

*a disposable piping/pastry bag
(optional)*

*a 6-hole muffin pan, lined with
foil cupcake cases*

## Makes 6

To make the nougat, put all of the ingredients in a food processor and blend until smooth. Fill the muffin cases about one-third full and put in the freezer to set for 20 minutes.

To make the caramel, soak the dates in 375 ml/1½ cups water for at least 2 hours, or ideally overnight. Drain the dates in a colander, then put in a food processor with the coconut oil. Blend until smooth and pour into a piping/pastry bag, or a sandwich bag.

Cut the bottom corner off the piping/pastry or sandwich bag and squeeze a circle of caramel into each cup.

Melt the dark/bittersweet chocolate by putting it in a heatproof bowl set over a saucepan or pot of simmering water. Take care not to let any water splash into the melting chocolate as it will seize up. Alternatively, put the chocolate in a heatproof bowl and heat in the microwave in bursts of 30 seconds, stirring between each burst of heat. Chocolate burns very easily so make sure you clean the sides of the bowl down as you go.

Pour the melted chocolate over the caramel and top with crushed nuts.

Freeze again for at least 15 minutes, until set.

---

### NUTRITIONAL INFORMATION
**Per cup:** 529 kcals/2206 kJ, 32 g fat (12.9 g saturated),
15.2 g protein, 41.6 g carbs (40.6 g sugars), trace salt, 6.8 g fibre

# Green Tea and Mango Cheesecake

I'm not someone who loves simple tastes; there always needs to be zing and brightness, or spice and stimulation to make it exciting for me. And why not? The tart and tangy combination of mango and green tea glaze adds a whole new dimension to creamy cheesecake. And you can steal this flavour pairing for smoothies and shakes too!

## Base

250 g/1½ cups almonds
165 g/1½ cups coconut flour
1 tablespoon pure vanilla extract
1 tablespoon granulated stevia
5–6 tablespoons coconut oil

## Filling

375 g/3 cups pine nuts
freshly squeezed juice of 2 large lemons
1 heaped tablespoon nutritional yeast
½ teaspoon salt
1 mango, peeled, stoned/pitted and roughly chopped
255 g/¾ cup raw honey (or use agave or maple syrup)

## Sauce

2 teaspoons matcha (green tea) powder
1 teaspoon non-dairy milk (such as almond, soy, or cocunut milk)

*a 20-cm/8-inch round springform pan, greased and lined with baking parchment*

## Serves 10–12

Begin by preparing the pine nuts for the filling. Put them in a small bowl and cover with water. Leave to soak for at least 2 hours, or ideally overnight. Drain the nuts, rinse well and set aside.

Put all of the base ingredients in a food processor and pulse until smooth. Line the bottom and sides of your prepared springform pan with the mixture, and put in the freezer to set while you prepare the filling.

Rinse the food processor and add the soaked pine nuts, lemon juice, nutritional yeast, salt, mango, and 170 g/½ cup of the raw honey (or agave or maple syrup). Blend until smooth.

Remove the pan from the freezer and pour in the filling.

Next, mix the matcha powder with the non-dairy milk and the remaining 85 g/¼ cup of raw honey (or agave or maple syrup) in a small bowl. Drizzle this mixture lightly onto the top of the cheesecake – you could use a chopstick or toothpick to swirl it into a pattern of your choice.

Put in the freezer for at least 45 minutes to set, and remove 20 minutes before serving.

The cheesecake will keep for up to 1 week if stored in the freezer, or 3 days in the fridge.

---

### NUTRITIONAL INFORMATION

**Per serving:** (if using honey) 629 kcals/ 2611 kJ, 47.9 g fat (10 g saturated), 16.8 g protein, 27.9 g carbs (24.3 g sugars), 0.4 g salt, 8.4 g fibre

# TURBO COOKIES

These cookies will keep you fuelled and energized in a bite. They're also an easy way to eat a protein-rich breakfast if eating nuts or even chicken at 9am is your idea of a nightmare. I would eat 3 for breakfast or 1–2 as a mid-morning or post-workout snack. Get creative by adding in things like goji berries, coconut pieces, spirulina, or nuts and seeds. If you want something a bit more indulgent, throw in a handful of dark/bittersweet chocolate chips.

90 g/$^2$/$_3$ cup almond meal
2 scoops protein powder (see page 4 for information on serving sizes)
150 g/$^2$/$_3$ cup almond butter
115 g/$^1$/$_3$ cup honey (or use agave or maple syrup)
1 tablespoon maca powder
$^1$/$_2$ teaspoon pink Himalayan salt
$^1$/$_2$ teaspoon ground cinnamon
1 teaspoon pure vanilla extract
*a baking sheet, greased and lined with baking parchment*

MAKES 8

Mix all of the ingredients together in a large mixing bowl.

Press the dough together and roll into a log with your hands. Cut flat discs about 4–5 cm/1$^1$/$_2$–2 inches wide and 1 cm/$^3$/$_8$ inch thick using a sharp knife and smooth the edges by hand.

Arrange the cookies on the prepared baking sheet and freeze for 20 minutes before transferring them to the fridge to store.

> **NUTRITIONAL INFORMATION**
> Per cookie: 262 kcals/1089 kJ, 17 g fat
> (1.3 g saturated), 11.3 g protein, 14.3 g carbs
> (12.5 g sugars), 0.5 g salt, 2.8 g fibre

# Chai-ginger Panna Cotta

I use chai and ginger together in so many different recipes because it's such an irresistible pairing. Here, I've used it to give an old classic a modern twist. I use agar as a thickener, but you could use Irish moss or gelatin, if you'd rather.

1 teaspoon agar powder
375 ml/1½ cups coconut milk
115 g/⅓ cup maple syrup
1 teaspoon pure vanilla extract
1 teaspoon chai spice
½ tablespoon grated fresh ginger

2 tablespoons coconut oil
1 banana, thinly sliced
2 tablespoons coconut sugar
a pinch of ground cinnamon
½ tablespoon freshly squeezed lemon juice

*4 ramekins*

## To Serve

4 tablespoons coconut chips

## Serves 4

Gently whisk the agar with 125 ml/½ cup of the coconut milk in a small saucepan or pot. Set over a medium heat and simmer gently for 3–5 minutes to dissolve the agar, taking care not to let the mixture boil. Once dissolved, stir in the remaining coconut milk, the maple syrup, vanilla extract, chai spice and ginger. Warm through for about 5 minutes.

Pour the mixture into the ramekins and put in the fridge to cool and set for at least 4 hours.

Before serving, toast the coconut chips in a dry frying pan/skillet set over a medium heat, until browned. Transfer to a plate to cool, then, using the same pan, warm the coconut oil. When the coconut oil begins to bubble, add the sliced banana to the pan and throw in the coconut sugar and cinnamon. Cook for 2–3 minutes to caramelize the banana.

Remove the panna cottas from the fridge, flip them over onto dessert plates and top with the caramelized banana and toasted coconut chips.

Add the lemon juice to the pan, stir and pour over the panna cottas.

---

**NUTRITIONAL INFORMATION**
Per serving: 329 kcals/1374 kJ, 18.5 g fat (16 g saturated),
1.8 g protein, 36.3 g carbs (33.3 g sugars), 0.3 g salt, 3.7 g fibre

# Caveman Ice Cream Sandwiches

Ice cream sandwiches are the one thing I just can't resist! These cherry-chocolate ones are basically the Fred Flintstone version – fruit, nuts, coconut oil and cacao only. When we eat simple foods like these, which our bodies can easily recognize, weight gain and health problems are off the table, because our bodies know exactly how to process them and use them as fuel. Pass me another!

## Cookie
250 g/1½ cups almonds
150 g/1½ cups dates
30 g/¼ cup raw cacao powder
1 tablespoon coconut oil

## Ice Cream
2 frozen bananas (see page 22)
a large handful of frozen cherries
    (see page 22)
a pinch of salt

*a baking sheet, greased and
    lined with baking parchment*

## Makes 8

Put all of the cookie ingredients in a food processor and pulse until smooth and a ball starts to form. Spread out to about 2½ cm/1 inch thick on the prepared baking sheet. Put in the freezer to set for at least 20 minutes. Remove from the freezer once it has hardened and cut into 16 small squares.

Rinse the food processor and pulse all of the ice cream ingredients together until they resemble the texture of ice cream.

Scoop 2 heaped tablespoons of ice cream onto half of the cookie squares and top each with another cookie, so that you have 6 sandwiches. Press the cookies together and use a knife to smooth out the ice cream filling, if necessary.

Store the sandwiches in the freezer until you are ready to serve, removing 5–10 minutes before serving.

> ### NUTRITIONAL INFORMATION
> **Per sandwich:** 275 kcals/1142 kJ, 19.7 g fat (3.1 g saturated),
> 9.4 g protein, 14.1 g carbs (12.4 g sugars), 0.2 g salt, 1.5 g fibre

# Super-easy Watermelon Sorbet

This little-known shortcut to making fruit sorbets is one of the coolest things I've discovered. I've made sorbets with all kinds of berries, peaches and mangoes, but this watermelon version is especially cute with the addition of chocolate chips to mimic the seeds.

**600 g/3 cups diced watermelon**

**a sprig of fresh mint (optional), plus extra to serve**

**75 g/½ cup chocolate chips**

**240 g/1 cup salt**

**2 cups ice cubes**

*an electric juicer*

*2 sandwich or freezer bags, 1 much larger than the other*

## Serves 2–4

Juice the watermelon and mint (if using) in an electric mixer. Pour 250 ml/ 1 cup of the juice into the small sandwich bag and close.

Combine the salt and ice in the large bag, then place the small sandwich bag inside. Close the large sandwich bag and shake it really hard; the watermelon juice will turn into sorbet!

Remove the watermelon sorbet from the bag, transfer to an airtight container and put in the freezer while you repeat the process with the remaining juice.

Once you have made the sorbet, stir through the chocolate chips to resemble the watermelon pips.

Garnish with mint and serve immediately or store in the freezer for up to 1 week.

> **NUTRITIONAL INFORMATION**
> **Per serving:** 291 kcals/1221 kJ,
> 11.4 g fat (6.6 g saturated), 3.2 g protein,
> 43 g carbs (42.7 g sugars), trace salt,
> 1.7 g fibre

# Banana Split

This dessert gained popularity in America during the early 1900s, when soda fountain bars competed to outdo eachother with elaborate sundae creations. The dish is designed to be shared, which to me is one of the best parts about eating in the first place.

## Whipped Coconut Cream

200 ml/¾ cup full-fat coconut milk

3 tablespoons stevia

## Ice Cream

4 frozen bananas (see page 22)

2 tablespoons cacao powder

½ tablespoon spirulina

1 tablespoon pistachios

5 strawberries

## Chocolate Sauce

2 tablespoons coconut oil

2 tablespoons cacao powder

1 tablespoon stevia

## To Assemble

1 banana, peeled

1 heaped tablespoon dried mulberries

## Makes 1 and Serves 2

Place the cans of coconut milk in the fridge for at least 8 hours or overnight; this will solidify the healthy coconut fats and separate them from the liquid.

Once chilled, open the cans and carefully scoop off the 'cream' that has risen to the top, discarding the liquid at the bottom. Put it in a large mixing bowl with the stevia, whip to stiff peaks with an electric whisk and set in the fridge until ready to serve.

To make the ice cream, pulse the frozen bananas in a food processor, until smooth. Divide the mixture into thirds, pulse one third with the cacao powder, transfer to an airtight container and freeze; pulse another third with the spirulina, transfer to an airtight container, mix in the pistachios and freeze; then pulse the remaining third with the strawberries, transfer to an airtight container and freeze.

To make the chocolate sauce, melt the coconut oil in a saucepan or pot set over a medium heat, then stir in the cacao powder and stevia.

To assemble, cut the fresh banana in half lengthwise and place the halves on either side of a serving dish. Scoop the three different ice cream flavours into balls and nestle them in between the banana slices, then top with the whipped coconut cream and the dried mulberries. Drizzle with chocolate sauce and serve.

> **NUTRITIONAL INFORMATION**
> **Per half split:** 500 kcals/2093 kJ, 22.8 g fat (16.2 g saturated), 10.8 g protein, 58.2 g carbs (49.3 g sugars), 0.6 g salt, 8.7 g fibre

# Mint-Chip Shake and Popsicle

This shake is healthy enough to drink for breakfast but so indulgent-tasting that it's also a great dessert. I regularly drink this and pour any leftover mixture into ice lolly moulds for when I feel like something sweet after dinner.

500 ml/2 cups almond milk
100 ml/⅓ cup full-fat coconut milk
2 frozen bananas (see page 22)
30 g/½ cup spinach, fresh or frozen
15 g/½ cup kale (stems only), fresh or frozen
6 mint leaves, fresh or frozen

2 teaspoons stevia (optional)
3 tablespoons cacao nibs, plus extra to serve
*a high-speed blender*

## Serves 2

Place the cans of coconut milk in the fridge for at least 8 hours or overnight; this will solidify the healthy coconut fats and separate them from the liquid.

Once chilled, open the cans and carefully scoop off the 'cream' that has risen to the top, discarding the liquid at the bottom.

Combine the almond milk, coconut milk, bananas, spinach, kale and mint leaves, and stevia (if using) in a high-speed blender. Blend until completely smooth, then add the cacao nibs and blend a little – you want them to break into smaller pieces but still be visible.

Garnish the smoothie with a few extra cacao nibs and drink immediately or pour into ice lolly moulds and freeze for a healthy, indulgent treat.

> **NUTRITIONAL INFORMATION**
> **Per serving:** 360 kcals/1499 kJ, 20.7 g fat (12.3 g saturated), 6.4 g protein, 31.7 g carbs (29 g sugars), 0.5 g salt, 11.1 g fibre

# RESOURCES

## HEALTH FOOD STORES

The best way to start eating more healthily is to source good-quality, fresh ingredients. These are just a few of my favourite places to shop.

**Amazon**
www.amazon.co.uk
www.amazon.com

**Essential Living Foods**
3550 Hayden Avenue
Culver City, CA 90232
+1 (310) 319 1555
www.essentiallivingfoods.com

**Foods to Love**
Unit 102
14 Cumberland Avenue
London NW10 7QL
info@foodstolove.co.uk
www.foodstolove.co.uk

**Fresh Direct**
Charbridge Way
Bicester
Oxfordshire
OX26 4SW
+44 (0)1869 365 600
www.freshdirect.co.uk

**Goodness Direct**
South March
Daventry
Northants NN11 4PH
+44 (0)1327 701 579
info@goodnessdirect.co.uk
www.goodnessdirect.co.uk

**Longevity Warehouse**
+1 (805) 870 5756
support@longevitywarehouse
.com
www.longevitywarehouse
.com

**Ocado**
Freepost 13498
PO BOX 3 62
Hatfield AL9 7BR
+44 (0)345 656 1234
ocado@ocado.com
www.ocado.com

**Raw Living**
+44 (0)1243 523 335
melissa@rawliving.co.uk
www.rawliving.eu

**Trader Joe's**
263 S La Brea Ave
Los Angeles, CA 90036
(and nationwide)
+ 1 (323) 965 1989
www.traderjoes.com

**Whole Foods Market UK**
63–97 Kensington High Street
The Barkers Building
London W8 5SE
(and nationwide)
+44 (0)20 7368 4500
www.wholefoodsmarket.com

**Whole Foods Market USA**
7871 Santa Monica Blvd
West Hollywood, CA 90046
+1 (323) 848 4200
250 7th Ave
New York, NY 10001
+1 (212) 924 5969
(and nationwide)
www.wholefoodsmarket.com

## WEBSITES

These websites and blogs offer up-to-date information on both Paleo and veganism, as well as online communities of other people approaching healthy eating in a similar way.

**Fitsugar**
www.fitsugar.com

**Mind Body Green**
www.mindbodygreen.com

**Nom Nom Paleo®**
www.nomnompaleo.com

**Oh She Glows**
www.ohsheglows.com

**PaleOMG**
www.paleomg.com

**This Rawsome Vegan Life**
www.thisrawsomeveganlife
.com

**Whole9life**
www.whole9life.com

**Well+Good**
www.wellandgood.com

## BOOKS

For further information and recipes try reading these books.

**Choosing Raw**
Gena Hamshaw
(Da Capo Lifelong Books, 2014)

**Eat, Drink, and Be Vegan**
Dreena Burton
(Arsenal Pulp Press, 2007)

**It Starts With Food**
Dallas and Melissa Hartwig
(Victory Belt Publishing, 2014)

**The Oh She Glows Cookbook**
Angela Liddon
(Penguin, 2014)

**Veganomicon**
Isa Chandra Moskowitz
(Da Capo Lifelong Books, 2008)

# FURTHER NUTRITIONAL INFORMATION

**Strawberry Shake, page 22**
**Per serving:** 418 kcals/1752 kJ, 15.7 g fat (8.6 g saturated),
10.4 g protein, 53.9 g carbs (49.4 g sugars), 1.1 g salt, 9.9 g fibre

**Brussels Sprouts Crisps, page 42**
**Per serving:** 74 kcals/308 kJ, 4.2 g fat (0.7 g saturated),
3.3 g protein, 3.4 g carbs (2.6 g sugars), 0.7 g salt, 4.8 g fibre

**Beetroot/Beet Crisps, page 42**
**Per serving:** 50 kcals/210 kJ, 2.8 g fat (0.4 g saturated),
1.1 g protein, 4.5 g carbs (4.1 g sugars), 0.2 g salt, 1.6 g fibre

**Baked Jicama Fries, page 45**
**Per serving:** 111 kcals/460 kJ, 0.6 g fat (0.1 g saturated),
3 g protein, 15 g carbs (6.7 g sugars), 2 g salt, 16.5 g fibre

**Winter Spice Macaroons, page 53**
**Per macaroon:** 115 kcals/478 kJ, 7.7 g fat (6.3 g saturated),
1.9 g protein, 8.8 g carbs (7.5 g sugars), 0 g salt, 1.7 g fibre

**Apple and Cinnamon Macaroons, page 53**
**Per macaroon:** 86 kcals/354 kJ, 7.7 g fat (6.3 g saturated),
1.9 g protein, 1.1 g carbs (1.1 g sugars), 0 g salt, 1.8 g fibre

# INDEX

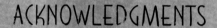

# ACKNOWLEDGMENTS

To my parents and siblings, it's a miracle I get anything done at all, because I could talk to you all day, every day and want for nothing. Thank you for seeing in me what I can't yet see, and nudging me towards it anyway. Special thanks to my 'momager' for reminding me that fun must *always* be had when working. Thank you to all my amazing clients for sharing your journeys with me; you are my true teachers. Thank you to all my extended family and friends for your never-ending enthusiasm and encouragement. Amelia, Nathalie and Sarah, thank you for the continuous surrogate sisterhood. To MP, thank you for inspiring me every day and reminding me what it's all about. To Zoe, thank you for being the living example of health, positivity and vitality. Your zest for life inspires me all over again every time I see you.

Thank you Cindy and Julia once again for your vision and enthusiasm. Our conceptual chats are always inevitably the most fun part of doing a book for me. To Sonya, thank you for lending your eyes to this project. I feel blessed to have been paired with you because the book only looks the way it does thanks to your stunning, simple and modern style. To Emily, thank you for making the food look beautiful. Your help along the way has been invaluable. To Clare, thank you for making me smile every day on set and inspiring me with your work ethic. To Stephanie, thank you for guidance and patience during the editing process. To Lauren, thank you for being so much fun to work with once again. Most importantly, to YOU, the reader: I hope every day brings you nothing less than vibrant health and joy, so that you can live your best life possible.